'67   '69   '73   '74

1967

- North American Aviation and Rockwell-Standard merge to form North American Rockwell with sales of $2.4 billion
- NAA's X-15 rocket-plane sets world speed record of 4,534 m.p.h., establishing new criteria for aerospace physics

1969

- First human steps on the moon, having been transported in North American Rockwell-built Apollo service and command modules and propelled by Rocketdyne engines.
- First communication from a man on the lunar surface to Earth, including first television pictures, were transmitted and received by Collins communications equipment
- North American Rockwell acquires the Miehle-Goss-Dexter company, which becomes Rockwell's Graphic Systems Division

'69

69

1970

- North American Rockwell is awarded the B-1 Advanced Technology Bomber program, which conducts its maiden flight in 1974

1973

- North American Rockwell changes its name to Rockwell International Corporation and acquires Collins Radio Company
- Rockwell wins U.S. Air Force contract for the first six of the new Global Positioning System satellites

1974

- Successful first flight of the B-1 bomber on December 23 marked the beginning of the phase one test program
- Rockwell was first valve manufacturer to submit a nuclear valve to seismic "shake" tests to simulate earthquake conditions
- Rockwell acquires Admiral Corporation, maker of major appliances/home entertainment products
- Rockwell awarded the original GPS Block I contract

1976

- On November 28, 1976, a Lockheed 1011 Tri-Star made the first automatic landing using a Collins automatic flight control system

1978

- The Boeing Airplane Company selects Collins avionics systems for its new-generation airliners — 757 and 767
- First launch of GPS Navstar I (Block I) satellite

1979

- U.S. Air Force awards $68 million contract for Collins to develop user equipment for Navstar Global Positioning System

1980

- President Ronald Reagan approves restarting B-1 bomber program after it was cancelled during Carter Administration

'81

1981

- Rockwell-built Space Shuttle Columbia is first launched

1983

- Rockwell opens Asheville, NC, axle manufacturing plant

67 68 69 70 71 72 73 74 75 76 77 78 79 80 81 82 83 84 85 86

LEADERSHIP

ROCKWELL

- Willard F. (Al) Rockwell, Jr., Chairman, '67–'79
- Robert (Bob) Anderson, Chairman & CEO, '79–'88
- J. Leland (Lee) Atwood, President & CEO, '67–'71
- Robert (Bob) Anderson, President & CEO, '71–'79
- Donald R. (Don) Beall, President & COO, '79–'88

AEROSPACE (Becomes part of Boeing, 1996.)

AUTOMOTIVE (Spun off as Meritor, Inc., 1997. Renamed ArvinMeritor, 2000.)

SEMICONDUCTORS (Spun off as Conexant, 1999.)

- Rockwell Semiconductors resulted in three public companies owned all or in part by Rockwell shareowners, Conexant, Skyworks and Mindspeed.
- Dwight W. Decker served as non-CEO/Chairman of Skyworks, '02–08', and continues to serve as non-CEO/Chairman of Mindspeed.
- Daniel A. (Dan) Artusi served as CEO of Conexant, '07–'08.
- D. Scott Mercer became Chairman & CEO of Conexant in '08.

COLLINS (Spun off as Rockwell Collins, 2001. Donald R. (Don) Beall served as non-CEO/Chairman for first year.)

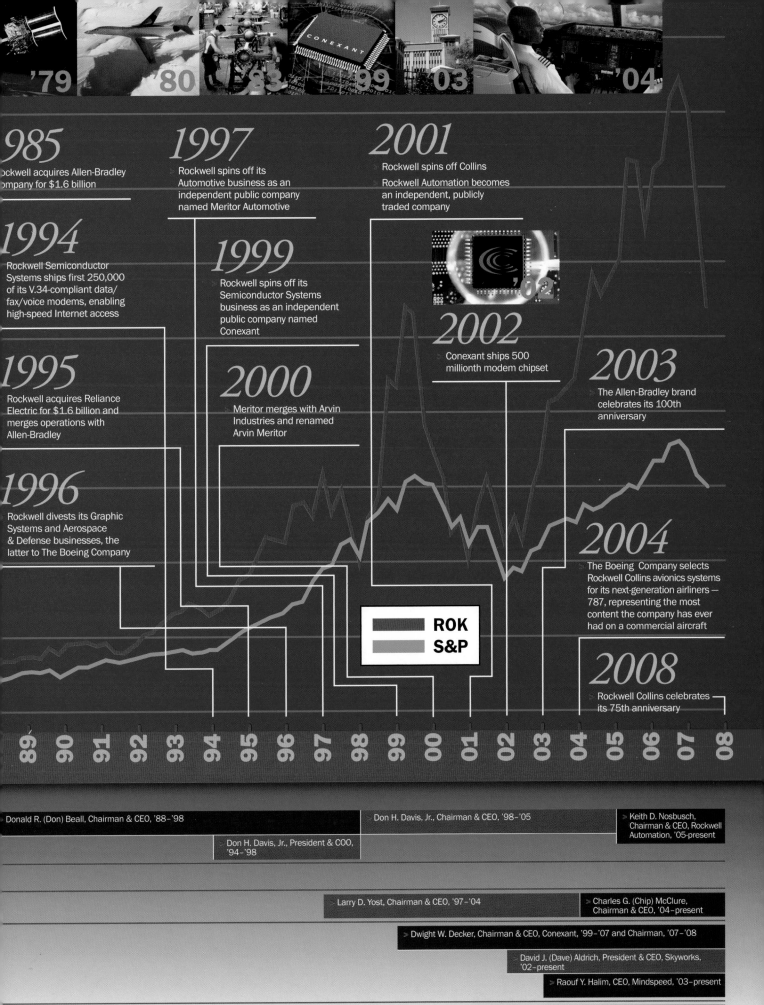

'79   '80   '83   '99   '03   '04

CONEXANT

1985
Rockwell acquires Allen-Bradley Company for $1.6 billion

1994
Rockwell Semiconductor Systems ships first 250,000 of its V.34-compliant data/fax/voice modems, enabling high-speed Internet access

1995
Rockwell acquires Reliance Electric for $1.6 billion and merges operations with Allen-Bradley

1996
Rockwell divests its Graphic Systems and Aerospace & Defense businesses, the latter to The Boeing Company

1997
Rockwell spins off its Automotive business as an independent public company named Meritor Automotive

1999
Rockwell spins off its Semiconductor Systems business as an independent public company named Conexant

2000
Meritor merges with Arvin Industries and renamed Arvin Meritor

2001
Rockwell spins off Collins

Rockwell Automation becomes an independent, publicly traded company

2002
Conexant ships 500 millionth modem chipset

2003
The Allen-Bradley brand celebrates its 100th anniversary

2004
The Boeing Company selects Rockwell Collins avionics systems for its next-generation airliners — 787, representing the most content the company has ever had on a commercial aircraft

2008
Rockwell Collins celebrates its 75th anniversary

ROK
S&P

89 90 91 92 93 94 95 96 97 98 99 00 01 02 03 04 05 06 07 08

Donald R. (Don) Beall, Chairman & CEO, '88–'98

Don H. Davis, Jr., President & COO, '94–'98

Don H. Davis, Jr., Chairman & CEO, '98–'05

Keith D. Nosbusch, Chairman & CEO, Rockwell Automation, '05–present

Larry D. Yost, Chairman & CEO, '97–'04

Charles G. (Chip) McClure, Chairman & CEO, '04–present

Dwight W. Decker, Chairman & CEO, Conexant, '99–'07 and Chairman, '07–'08

David J. (Dave) Aldrich, President & CEO, Skyworks, '02–present

Raouf Y. Halim, CEO, Mindspeed, '03–present

Clayton M. (Clay) Jones, President & CEO, '01–'02 and Chairman, President & CEO, '02–present

ISBN: 978-0-615-22738-2

Library of Congress Control Number: 2008908965

This book is printed on acid-free paper.

FORMATION, EVOLUTION AND TRANSFORMATION OF ROCKWELL

by Donald R. Beall

Table of Contents

Preface and Acknowledgements

"What happened to Rockwell?" is a question that I've been asked many times by many people – in the business community, educators, students, and the general public. Rockwell became a market-focused leader in important Aerospace, Automotive and Electronics global markets. Then in the mid-'90s, the Aerospace business was combined with Boeing, the Automotive business was established as a new public company, leaving the continuing Rockwell as a diversified leader in certain Electronics global markets. Those Electronic businesses have become five public companies.

The Rockwell shareowners who kept their stock through all these transactions have achieved very favorable results … that is the easy part of the story to tell. In many ways the more interesting part of the story is the thinking that led to the separation, the management philosophy and practices that were employed, and then a discussion of what happened to all of the derivative businesses. This book deals with all of that.

There were so many outstanding leaders over the years involved in the innovation and entrepreneurship that created these businesses that it is impossible to tell all their personal stories. The current leaders of the successor companies have assisted in telling this story. I would like to thank all those committed individuals from Rockwell's predecessor and successor companies – both active and retired – who have helped tell this story. Their contributions have been instrumental in publishing this book. I consider it an honor to have led these management teams and this company during its transformation and evolution periods.

I'd also like to thank the University of California, Irvine, The Paul Merage School of Business for their interest in helping me complete this project. I hope that the book serves to educate and inspire others.

Don Beall

Introduction

by Dean Andrew J. Policano

The Paul Merage School of Business, University of California, Irvine

The philosophy of the Don Beall Center for Innovation and Entrepreneurship is based on the well known premise that leading companies are leaders of innovation. Companies that sustain growth rates at the top of their industry are often the first to develop new products and processes; companies in decline are often followers who innovate more slowly than their competitive environment demands. Understanding the drivers of innovation is essential to successfully implement a strategy for obtaining sustainable growth. The vision of the Beall Center is to become a thought leader in the emerging area of strategic innovation as the key driver of sustainable growth.

The Merage School launched the Center for Innovation and Entrepreneurship in 2004 with a focus on research and programs to serve the business community and to study businesses and organizations that have grown successfully through strategic innovation. One company that truly stands out for its innovation in products, processes and business strategy is Rockwell International. The story of Rockwell's strategy and success is told within this book.

In June 2007, Rockwell Chairman/CEO Emeritus, Donald R. Beall and his family named the Center with a generous gift that will support path breaking research and vital educational programming. Don Beall is highly recognized for his leadership over many years in providing a sustained path of business growth based on innovative products and business models. We are indeed very grateful and honored to have the Center bear Don's name as a symbol of thought leadership in this critical area.

The Don Beall Center for Innovation and Entrepreneurship will be the vehicle through which a significant proportion of research and thought leadership on the newest and most influential approaches to strategic innovation will be completed and disseminated to the global business community. In addition, the Center will provide education for graduate students and researchers to understand the process of innovation and continues to present opportunities for entrepreneurs to benefit from the many resources the Center offers to startups and researchers with exciting new business ideas.

And, who better to illustrate this process than Don Beall himself – a captain of industry … an architect of change … a leader who champions the cause of "intra-preneurs" – men and women who innovate within large organizations … a businessman and community leader with high integrity, who believes that the culture and character of a company is derived from the character of its people – not vice versa.

In this book, Don Beall tells the story of the formation, evolution and transformation of Rockwell, one of America's greatest companies.

Don describes the heritage businesses that led to the formation of a diversified high-technology company with leadership businesses serving aerospace, electronics and automotive global markets; the evolution of these businesses into a diversified group of leadership electronics businesses serving factory automation, communications, avionics and various communications-semiconductor world markets; and, ultimately, the transformation of those electronics businesses into five public companies and how all of these strategic actions created significant shareowner value.

As any great leader will acknowledge, success such as this is made possible only with a strong management team. Don Beall is quick to credit his predecessors, his senior management team, and his successors in helping to achieve these accomplishments. During his tenure, Don's call to action to his team and to all Rockwell employees was consistent and clear:

"We need leaders at all levels committed to defining the future, making and changing rules, governing competition in our markets, and becoming architects of innovation and growth. I ask each of you to take on the mantle of personal leadership wherever you work within Rockwell and in everything you do."

These words reflected Don's philosophy and commitment and that of his predecessors and successors. It was the strategic implementation of this shared vision and philosophy that resulted in the successful transformation of Rockwell. You will read more about this team effort within this book.

The culmination of this transformation effort under Don's leadership was recognized by his peers at the time of his retirement from Rockwell.

> *"Your leadership at Rockwell International Corporation is certainly leaving a rich heritage."*
> *– Stephen D. Bechtel, Jr., chairman emeritus, Bechtel Group*

> *"You leave with the realization that you completely revamped the strategy of the company, something that doesn't often happen. Congratulations on a job well done."*
> *– Lawrence A. Bossidy, chairman and CEO, AlliedSignal*

> *"Congratulations on your superb leadership and visionary accomplishments at Rockwell."*
> *– Herbert D. Kelleher, president and CEO, Southwest Airlines*

> *"Very rarely and almost never as successfully, can current management restructure a company as well as you did. The growth in earnings and market capitalization speak eloquently of your achievements."*
> *– Richard M. Rosenberg, chairman and CEO – retired, BankAmerica Corporation*

> *"You should be very proud of creating one of the best transformations in business."*
> *– John F. Welch, chairman and CEO, General Electric*

Don believes very strongly in the value of higher education as crucial to the innovation and entrepreneurial process that will lead to a stronger America. He has volunteered his expertise to UC Irvine's Merage School, the Samueli School of Engineering, the Beall Center for Art and Technology within the School of the Arts, the UC Irvine Chief Executive Round Table, and the California Institute for Telecommunications and Information Technology.

In this spirit of innovation and entrepreneurship, and in order to preserve the historical significance of Rockwell, its predecessor companies, and their people, Don has volunteered to share his story of Rockwell. His forward-thinking style of leadership closely mirrors the mission and objectives of the Don Beall Center for Innovation and Entrepreneurship.

Read on … there is much to be learned from this great American leader and how he has given new meaning to the phrase, "the art and science of strategic innovation."

Dean Andrew J. Policano
and the Merage School family

The Formation, Evolution and Transformation of Rockwell

In the fall of 1967, two very dissimilar major American corporations merged – North American Aviation and Rockwell-Standard. North American was a leading aerospace contractor, and Rockwell was a leading producer of automotive and truck components. This merger occurred during the period when many major conglomerates were formed (ITT, Raytheon, TRW, Textron, Teledyne, etc.). The Company, initially named North American Rockwell, proceeded over the next several years to acquire many additional businesses, very much in the conglomeration/diversification mode. The major businesses added were power tools, gas and water meters, specialized industrial valves, newspaper printing presses, textile machinery, consumer appliances, avionics and telecommunication, yachts, factory automation controls, and a host of smaller stand-alone businesses.

By the early 1990s, Rockwell had become a diversified high-technology company very much focused on aerospace, electronics, and automotive markets. Through a series of strategic transactions, the aerospace business is now part of the Boeing Company, and the automotive and electronics businesses have become all or part of six public companies. The value to the Rockwell shareowner that resulted from these transactions has been a return over the last 30 years of about 16 percent, compounded, as of September 2007. (That value at August 31, 2008, with the weak economy and volatile stock market is 14 percent.)

Why is this story being told?

Rockwell is a company whose leaders and products and services have great historical significance, not just for the company but also for the nation and American industry, as you will read in the coming pages. Throughout its formation, evolution and transformation, Rockwell has evolved: (1) a business point of view that encouraged creativity, innovation and a spirit of entrepreneurialism; (2) a form of management that involved all levels of management and employees; and (3) a series of great leaders who challenged the status quo both in the predecessor companies and continue to do so in the successor companies. The contributions and spirit of these great leaders – named and unnamed – are captured within this story and are evident in the shareowner value that was created along the way.

The idea behind this book is not to write a detailed history of the company. Instead, it is intended to:

- Briefly describe the major companies that came together to become Rockwell;
- Illustrate the change in composition of the company over three decades;
- Discuss the importance of the management processes and values employed within Rockwell and its Vision and Credo, and how the people of Rockwell implemented the action strategies and attitudes of the Rockwell Vision;
- Describe the planning and thoughts that led to the decision to place the aerospace business with The Boeing Company;

Origin of North American Aviation (NAA)

- 1928 – incorporated as a holding company
- 1934 – Operations begun in Dundalk, MD (NA-16/BT-9 – NAA's first aircraft wins an Air Corps trainer competition)
- 1935 – moved to Inglewood, CA, establishes full-scale production facility, and ventures into advanced aeronautics.
- NAA plays vital role in two wars and achieves America's first entry into space.

- Discuss the ultimate separation of the Automotive and Electronics businesses into several public companies;

- Recap what has occurred since the separation with each of the resulting entities;

- Show the financial impact to the Rockwell shareowner.

North American Aviation Post-War ...

- Military aircraft contracts abruptly terminated after the war.
- NAA plants were closed; employment fell from a peak of 92,000 to 5,000.
- NAA rejects commercial products as a means to post-war recovery and maintains efforts in military aircraft and new technologies of the missile.
- NAA led into the jet age with its FJ Fury series, B-45 Tornado – the first Air Force multi-engine jet bomber – and F-86 Sabre Jet – the first swept-wing jet fighter that achieved a 10-to-1 kill ratio over the Soviet built MiG-15 during the Korean War. A total of 8,681 F-86 Sabre Jets were produced by NAA and under license.
- NAA designed the F-100 Super Sabre (follow-on to F-86). Known as the Hun, the F-100, would become the first operational supersonic fighter for the Air Force.
- The first "Wild Weasel" aircraft utilizing the two-seat F-100F variant was developed in the early 1960s. This highly classified program, known as SEAD (Suppression of Enemy Air Defenses), utilized electronic black boxes and anti-radiation missiles to defeat enemy SAM sites. This vital mission is still carried out today using the F-16CJ.
- F-100s also served in many foreign air forces, and a total of 2,294 were built.
- For the U.S. Navy, NAA produced the nuclear-capable carrier-based AJ Savage bomber/reconnaissance series, and the supersonic RA-5C Vigilante reconnaissance aircraft. Ahead of its time, the RA-5C was able to transmit real-time mission telemetry back to the carrier.
- NAA's aeronautical expertise excelled rapidly with the development XB-70 Valkyrie tri-sonic bomber for the Air Force. Using variable-geometry inlets and compression lift, the XB-70 was able to achieve sustained Mach 3+ flight at altitudes above 70,000 feet.
- Other production aircraft included the T-28 Trojan, T-2 Buckeye and T-39 training aircraft. The T-39 used by the USAF, U.S. Navy and U.S. Marine Corps, led to the Sabreliner business jet series. Many other experimental fighters and bombers were developed in the post-war period.

1. F-86 Sabre Jets downed 600 MiGs in confirmed kills, plus 143 probably kills during Korean War air battles – a kill ratio of nearly 10-to-1 *(Photo by Erik Simonsen)*

2. World War II Production:
   17,000 T-6 Trainers *(pictured, Boeing archives)*
   15,000 P-51 Fighters,
   10,000 B-25 Bombers

3. WASPs – In August 1943, the Women's Air Force Service Pilots (WASPs) were formed to carry out the vital task of ferrying combat aircraft to the war zone. Here WASPs receive a pre-flight briefing before taking off in the NAA AT-6 Texan. *(USAF photo – Bill Yenne collection)*

4. B-25 Bomber – NAA designed the tremendously successful B-25 Mitchell medium bomber. The B-25 was chosen for the Doolittle Raid on Japan that launched from an aircraft carrier. Nearly 10,000 B-25s were produced during the peak war years. *(Rockwell International photo)*

5. P-51 Mustang – The NAA P-51D Mustang was considered the most aerodynamically efficient fighter built during World War II. *(Photo by Erik Simonsen)*

6. Nautilus – From the control room of the Nautilus, the U.S. Navy's first nuclear-powered submarine, crewmembers observe the first transit under the North Pole. The Autonetics N-6 guidance system, derived from the Navaho missile program guided the Nautilus. *(U.S. Navy photo)*

7. Navaho configuration consisted of a booster and piggyback vehicle that first flew as the X-10. A precursor to today's cruise missile, the Navaho leaves a legacy of technology transition to other programs. *(Rockwell International photo)*

8. Hound Dog – A precursor to today's cruise missiles, the NAA GAM-77 Hound Dog air-to-ground missile greatly enhanced the effectiveness of the B-52s serving in Strategic Air Command. Re-designated AGM-28 in 1963, the Hound Dog remained in service for 17 years. *(USAF Photo)*

9. X-15 – Regarded as the most successful X-plane in history, the NAA X-15 manned hypersonic rocket plane reached Mach 6.7 (4,520 mph) and an altitude of 254,000 feet during its 199 test flights. *(NASA photo)*

10. Apollo – In the time period when project Mercury was operational and Gemini program was being developed, in a bold stroke, NASA awarded NAA the Apollo contract on November 28, 1961. NAA designed and built the Command/ Service Modules (CSM). Apollo CSM brought the first astronauts to the moon for the first lunar landing on July 20, 1969. (NASA photo)

Aerospace ...

- 1950 – Navaho missile weapon system development
- 1956 - NAA created a number of divisions focused on rocket engines, missiles, electronics, nuclear energy, space and aircraft. All were supported by a world-class Science Center.
  - Rocketdyne Division produced rocket engines for the Redstone, Jupiter C/Jupiter launch vehicle/IRBM (Intermediate Range Ballistic Missile), Navaho, Atlas ICBM (Intercontinental Ballistic Missile), Thor IRBM, Delta rockets and Sidewinder and Sparrow air-to-air missile programs.
  - Space and Missile Division produced nuclear-armed Hound Dog unmanned air-to-ground guided missile for the B-52 – truly a predecessor to the cruise missiles of today.
  - Electronics Division (Autonetics) was a leader in the flight computers, flight control, and inertial navigators for the Minuteman ICBM. All inertial navigators for nuclear submarine fleet were developed and produced by Autonetics.
  - Autonetics develops very advanced digital avionics, navigation, and radar systems.
  - The company developed the famous X-15 hypersonic rocket-powered airplane and, subsequently, won the Apollo Command/Service Module contract.
  - Company also developed and built the second stage of Saturn V (the Apollo launch vehicle), and the J-2 and F-1 rocket engines that powered every stage of the 363 ft. Saturn V.
  - A rich set of electronic technologies underlie these great programs and would be a catalyst for much innovation and entrepreneurial activity in the new company.

FORMATION – THE PREDECESSOR COMPANIES

North American Aviation

North American Aviation has a rich history: military aircraft, missiles, space vehicles, rocket propulsion, nuclear technology, avionics, inertial navigation, flight control, and supporting technologies. These capabilities and accomplishments are outlined in the sidebar summaries. Much more information exists in various historical books referenced at the end of this document.

Rockwell-Standard

Rockwell-Standard was a very different company, rooted in Midwest industrial America. It had been formed through a series of mergers by Col. Willard Rockwell, the father of Willard F. (Al) Rockwell, who was the chairman and CEO of Rockwell-Standard at the time of the merger.

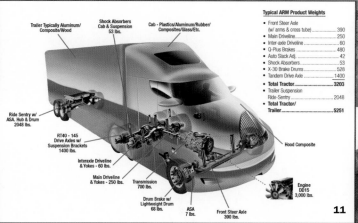

11 12 13

The predecessor companies that ultimately became Rockwell-Standard included elements of The Timken Company – manufacturers of axles for wagons and carriages (late 19th century). With the invention of the Timken tapered bearing in 1899, the company found itself in two growing but different businesses. After moving both businesses to Canton, Ohio, in 1902 to be close to the automobile industry, Henry and William R. Timken split the business in 1909. The axle business became The Timken Detroit Axle Company (TDA), which specialized in heavy-duty axles. With the Timken name on the axle, the bearing company found it virtually impossible to sell bearings to other axle builders. This posed a significant problem. In 1925, Timken-Detroit moved to specialize on heavy-duty axles. Four years later, TDA acquired The Wisconsin Parts Company, an axle maker, owned by Col. Rockwell, who later became president of TDA. In 1936, TDA acquired The Standard Steel Spring Company and, in 1953, TDA and Standard Steel were merged to become Rockwell Spring and Axle. In 1958, the company became Rockwell-Standard — one of the predecessor companies that formed North American Rockwell. The Timken name was gone, but the family remained among the largest Rockwell-Standard shareowners.

Rockwell-Standard's primary businesses were in the automotive supply arena. Primary products were heavy-duty axles, brakes, suspension components and other products for heavy trucks and off-highway vehicles. Additionally, there were numerous products supplying the light vehicle market, including wheels, springs, drivelines, bumpers, suspension components and wheel covers. The company also was involved in general aviation through the Aero-Commander business, producing single and twin-engine aircraft, including a very popular line of turbo-prop aircraft.

Rockwell-Standard was seeking the technology resources of North American with the idea of commercialization, and North American was seeking diversification.

11. ArvinMeritor Commercial Vehicle Systems axle and braking systems*

12. ArvinMeritor Light Vehicle Systems Detroit Michigan facility's quality components including roof systems*

13. ArvinMeritor off-highway products for specialty vehicles*

* Rockwell Standard's automotive operations later became the public company ArvinMeritor

14. Front page of internal Rockwell publication, "Los Angeles Skywriter," announcing NAA merger with Rockwell-Standard

Flying Families

The Timken's and the Rockwell's became close over many years. Louise (an avid pilot) and Henry H. Timken, Jr. had no children, and it was often said that aviation became their family. They had the first non-military jet in the United States: a French trainer called a Maurane-Salinier. A little-known fact is that Henry Timken encouraged the Rockwell's to consider merging with North American.

The Evolution – Focused Aerospace, Electronics, and Automotive Businesses

15. Among Admiral's full line of major appliances were an Imperial Duplex, no-defrosting freezer-refrigerator.

16. Consumer Products Group – jig saw and drill

During the period 1967-1996, the company went through many phases that resulted in three very focused business areas: Aerospace, Electronics, and Automotive. Along the way, there were many other businesses that were acquired and subsequently divested – those businesses are described briefly below.

Rockwell Manufacturing was acquired in 1973; it was comprised of leadership businesses in high-performance valves for industrial, power generation, and energy markets. It also had a leading business in industrial power tools, as well as very good businesses in commercial and residential gas and water meters.

That same year, the Admiral Corporation was acquired with businesses in home appliances, both white goods (refrigerators and laundry products) and brown goods (televisions and radio products).

The Miehle-Goss-Dexter company was acquired in this period; it was a leader in newspaper and certain commercial printing presses.

Several businesses serving textile machinery markets were acquired (looms, industrial sewing machines, and double-width knitting machines). A whole series of very unrelated acquisitions of small leading businesses in various industrial products and boating also were acquired during this period.

One grouping of industrial leading small businesses in 1975 became the first significant private equity leveraged buyout for Kohlberg Kravis Roberts & Co. In the various financial exhibits the impact of these businesses will be displayed. A very important aspect related to all of these businesses were the resources they provided to build the financial strength of the overall company; these businesses when sold provided significant cash necessary to build aerospace, electronics and automotive.

Each of these acquired businesses has a story all its own. They did not end up in the transformed Rockwell and will not be covered in detail in this book. Most were strong product lines and businesses with terrific people, solid market positions and leadership technology (valves, meters, industrial tools, filters, specialized bearings, industrial chain, mechanical controls, Admiral white goods, gears, etc.). Without exception, those businesses ended up as a part of larger, very focused organizations with significant technology, product, marketing, sales and distribution synergies.

One will see as we progress through this book, the very clear preference within Rockwell for the development of very market focused businesses. The objective then was to bring those very focused businesses to their full potential through aggressive global business strategies but with very clear market focus.

The balance of this book will focus on the development of what became the three primary Rockwell businesses: Aerospace, Electronics, and Automotive.

In 1996, the Aerospace business was sold to The Boeing Company, and the Rockwell share-owners received Boeing stock and cash. In 1997, the Automotive business was spun off as a new company owned by the Rockwell shareowners – Meritor, Inc. That left the continuing Rockwell as a major diversified electronics company.

Subsequently, in 1998, Rockwell spun off the Semiconductor business owned also by the Rockwell shareowners – Conexant, Inc. In 2001, the remaining Rockwell separated into two world leaders in their respective markets – Rockwell Automation and Rockwell Collins. All are owned by Rockwell shareowners.

The thinking that led to these strategic actions and the results will unfold in the pages to follow.

However, before we describe the evolution of the Aerospace, Electronics, and Automotive business, it will be helpful to provide a discussion of the importance of the management processes and values; and a financial overview of these businesses.

17. Rockwell SR Meters measure water usage for water utilities

18. Admiral 25-inch Super-Solarcolor, 100 percent solid-state television set

19. Rockwell operated the largest closed flow loop of its kind to test and develop high-volume gas measurement equipment

20. Goss Metroliner double-width web offset press

21. Rockwell Draper fabric flyshuttle loom

Management Processes and Values

A critical part of Rockwell's transformation was how the people themselves changed the culture and how the Rockwell Credo and Vision were developed and implemented.

Below is a discussion of how the management environment changed as the company prepared itself for the 21st Century.

Organizing for the 21st Century – Characterization of Rockwell's Changing Management Environment

In the 1980s, the company went through a lot of "traditional blocking and tackling" – de-layering the management structure to adjust to the declining aerospace and defense business and to simplify the operations for increasing global competition.

The New Paradigm

In the late '80s and '90s, Don Beall and his senior management team began to increase their efforts to transform the management approach, stressing the importance of "Integrative Management" – breaking down barriers between functions, line and staff and individuals. Don stated, "We have asked our employees for their hands; now, we need to ask for their hearts and minds to reach our full potential."

The organizational structure evolved from a hierarchical, silo-based structure with many levels into a more flat, more flexible, team-based environment. Management style transformed from one resembling a command-and-control, need-to-know communications basis to a more participative, employee involved, and expanded communications style. The role of corporate staff changed from a more operational and sometimes controlling nature to a more strategic, coaching and mentoring relationship with the businesses. Engineering functions raised expectations of first-time successes vs. the traditional model of building two or three successive prototypes. Awareness of customer acceptance and expectation of quality products and services increased significantly. People became viewed more as assets than as expenses. Training was used as a competitive lever, and teams vs. individuals focused on final products and overall processes rather than narrowly defined jobs.

Ad hoc management mechanisms were put in place to allow more than 30 divisions and tens of thousands of people to operate under Rockwell's four core business areas to share technology among themselves; to have a very good awareness of what was going on in each other's operation; and to know how to seek assistance if their businesses needed help.

Examples of these management mechanisms included:

- Product Integrity Committee
- Research Steering Committee
- Technical Advisory Committee
- Productivity Group
- Human Resources Advisory Board

Management Principles

In addition, the following set of Selected Management Principles for running the corporation was formulated, including establishing a company vision.

Selected Management Principles

Establishing a clear and concise company vision and core values around which all people can relate;

Strong, internal communications on business objectives and core values at all levels;

A corporate staff that is organized and staffed around the core competencies that add real value to the business/corporation – a staff that is focused on bringing out the maximum potential of each business, profitable growth, and enhanced shareowner value;

Global growth will be a major objective of each of our businesses – with particular focus on growing the service/after-market segment;

Business units that link themselves with other Rockwell businesses to maximize growth and competitive advantage;

Few or no layers of management between the profit generators and the business unit president. In-depth staffs will exist at only one of three levels within Rockwell business units (i.e., sector, group, division/plant);

Accountability: decision-making positioned at the lowest practical level; Focus is placed on the high value added core functions of the business, with support/service functions being pooled or purchased from the outside;

High utilization of self-managed, cross-functional teams;

High utilization of non-permanent employees for peak loads;

Emphasis on continual learning, innovation, and networking across businesses;

Reward and recognition programs linked to team and business objective

accomplishments. Incentive systems that reward profitable growth, shareowner value, and leadership behavior down to the lowest practical level in the company;

Flexible organization structures and management teams that quickly adjust to support business strategy and customer needs;

Flexible work arrangements;

Frequent surveys for customer and employee feedback.

The Rockwell Vision

To be THE best

diversified

high-tech company

in the world.

All of this was part of a master plan on how the management team would transform the new Rockwell into a higher performing company with high employee enthusiasm and commitment to goals – even in the face of a declining aerospace market and increasing global competition.

Involving the senior management team and employees in a more participative style of management allowed the company to present a stronger image of Rockwell as a diverse but well-integrated company. It enhanced the awareness of Rockwell and its proud heritage and strong network of capabilities that were brought to bear to customers and shareowners worldwide.

All of the successor businesses benefited from the values and progressive management practices employed throughout Rockwell during the '80s and '90s. The Rockwell Vision and Credo were very important components of this management transformation.

Rockwell Vision and Credo

Prior to the rollout of the Vision, changes in the management environment had started coming about in late 1980s and the early 1990s. A conceptual framework had been developed as to how the new Rockwell moving forward needed to shape its management style and operating environment for a high-performance company in the coming years. The focus was to unleash the full power potential of the people at all levels of the company.

In 1994, the Rockwell Vision statement and Credo were rolled out following a decade-long evolutionary process that involved numerous meetings of general managers, staff heads, and more than 400 employee focus groups.

The overarching vision statement agreed to was the following statement:

To be THE best diversified high-tech company in the world.

"Not ONE of the best. THE best," said Beall, when introducing the Vision statement at a company-wide management meeting.

Beall and his team were consistent in clearly communicating the Credo and Vision over a period of time and through many mediums. "The culture and character of a company is derived from the character of its people – not vice versa," said Beall.

He described the need for effective new strategies and tactics in order to address the globalization of competition, including: replacing bureaucracy with teamwork; replacing turf wars with cooperation; improving processes, productivity and products; focusing on the customer like never before and involving them in the design of Rockwell's solutions to their issues; emphasis on self-managed teams and high performance work teams; and moving rapidly to high-performance work systems.

These strategies and tactics were embedded in the words and the principles in the Rockwell Credo and Vision statements. The Vision laid out specific Action Strategies and Attitudes, which Rockwell employees would implement in their everyday work processes and which were judged by customers, employees, shareowners and the community.

During the process of integrating these Action Strategies and Attitudes throughout the company, Beall challenged his management team and all Rockwell employees to continue to take the next step.

That next step, for many, was a giant leap.

A "small business mentality" was employed ... every employee was encouraged to feel accountable for their entire business, not just their immediate job. That was facilitated with considerable top-down communication on the performance of the overall business segment, its customers, its competitors, and leveling with the entire team on the performance of the business. Top corporate management was sufficiently involved in the strategic planning of every business, so that when the process was over, it always resulted in a "we" plan ... not a "we versus they" plan. They encouraged sharing best practices to minimize the bureaucratic tendencies of large organizations.

Rockwell had a reputation for outstanding performance. The company employed a sophisticated strategic and financial planning system, including leading-edge program planning and control systems required for the large government programs. High standards of business conduct training occurred throughout the company. The company had its own management training school and encouraged continuous learning. Succession planning and manpower development was an important part of the management process. Innovation and entrepreneurialism were encouraged.

"Levers for change" were introduced within the organization. For example, teams of senior people comprised the Management Process Task Force. This task force tested every process, every function to ensure alignment to the Rockwell Vision and Credo.

Extensive employee surveys were created and implemented, including a "360-degree" survey that had employees rating, among other items, the performance of their own managers with respect to the principles and values of the Rockwell Vision and Credo.

These changes and innovative practices were communicated internally between divisions. Several vehicles – including high performance work teams and systems – were used to ensure that cohesive, effective management processes were initiated and shared as best practices.

In the new Rockwell, these high-performance, self-managed work teams shared responsibility for goal setting, task completion, quality, cycle time reductions, work schedule, job rotations, and other decision-making processes. Over a period of time, positive results were apparent in feedback from the four judges outlined in the Vision statement – customers, employees, shareowners and community.

Chairman's Team Award

In order to recognize and celebrate the successes of these self-managed work teams, the Chairman's Team Award was introduced in the early '90s and implemented throughout the company. These teams selected an area of focus consistent with the company's goals – be it a product or a service. Rockwell Collins continues this program with the following goals: superior customer value; sustained and profitable growth; global leadership in served markets; and talented and motivated people.

Specific objectives were developed by the entire team; and progress toward those goals and objectives was measured on a daily basis, with the idea that the contribution of each and every team member was critical for success. A healthy spirit of competition was felt throughout the company as teams were nominated for the Chairman's Team Award.

The Rockwell Chairman's Team Award was presented annually at major business unit locations to multiple teams by the chairman himself after viewing team results. The recognition provided an opportunity to honor the outstanding teams within the company in a ceremony amidst their management and peers. The award and celebration event also recognized teams for superior accomplishments that supported the Rockwell Vision. The teams exemplified sustaining core values and processes, and a willingness to set and attain breakthrough goals.

It is especially important to recognize that this award was open to teams throughout Rockwell — both domestic and international sites. The majority of teams also were cross-

22

22. The Rockwell Chairman's Team Award included three solid interlocking circles of red, green and blue that overlapped to form a rounded triangle and which represented the strong disciplines of business. Around the triangle shape were nine circles of individual colors intertwined, which represented the nine businesses of Rockwell International. A black base held the glass award and a recognition plaque for each winning team.

functional throughout the company, and everyone was encouraged to participate. The program lives on today within several of the businesses.

TECHNOLOGY INNOVATION

It was a well-recognized fact that Rockwell's strengths were founded on the technical innovations that came from the business units, and technical innovations came from people. To encourage this innovation, measurable goals were set forth for each business for a percent of their sales to come from new product introductions. This encouraged cross-functional and cross-business teams to leverage the best of their technologies and processes to spark innovation and new product introductions. The incentive compensation system also was adjusted with the goal of reinforcing behavior that would improve performance, productivity and innovation.

A. Engineering Recruitment

Rockwell was very active in ensuring that each business had a proactive college recruiting program, focused on those schools whose curriculum best matched the company's needs and from which Rockwell recruited new engineers.

There were two important goals of this concept: (1) It was critical that Rockwell have a pipeline of fresh-thinking technologists coming into the company; and (2) Technology moves so fast that once Rockwell hired these engineers, it was important to keep their skills current so as not to let them go stale. To keep them fresh and current in their relevant technologies and to keep the spirit of innovation alive, every engineer in the company was required to get at least 40 hours of training a year.

An average of 1,000 new engineers were recruited each year to join Rockwell, which had one of the largest college recruiting programs in American industry. In fact, Rockwell was recognized as one of the largest recruiters of technical talent in the country. The company's chief engineers played a key role in this program, visiting the universities, studying their curriculums, and helping shape and influence those curriculums to address the type and level of engineering skills that industry needed. The chief engineers looked at the schools that had the strongest, most advanced curriculums in technologies that Rockwell wanted to pursue. Rockwell then would recruit heavily from these schools. To further strengthen this strategic approach, scholarships and summer internships were targeted toward the students of these 10 key schools. Today, this key school concept continues in many of the Rockwell successor businesses.

B. Centers of Excellence for Competitive Advantage

Across the mix of Rockwell's diverse businesses, there was significant commonality in the development and use of many basic technologies, such as digital signal processing, linear and non-linear control logic, modeling and simulation technologies, etc. Similarly, across a subset of Rockwell businesses, there were commonalities in product components and subsystems that were integrated into higher level products or systems, such as power supplies, digital frequency synthesizers, cockpit subsystems, etc. At a higher level, within major business groups, there were product commonalities, such as GPS receivers, avionics displays, antenna systems, etc.

To minimize redundant development costs, to manage the critical mass of key engineers and technologists required for technical leadership, and to provide maximum sharing of innovative design approaches across the company, Rockwell used two simple management techniques.

One of these was to establish corporate or business unit "centers of excellence" to develop multi-use components, subsystems, or processes – displays, GPS receivers, antennas, as

D. R. Beall on Management Philosophy:

Since this book will be read and studied by graduate students, the following excerpts from Don Beall's commencement speech to the Class of 1987 at UCLA Anderson Graduate School of Management might be helpful. They are Don Beall's thoughts on values and management concepts. Don's son Ken Beall was a member of this graduating class.

"I believe strongly that the essence of managerial leadership is running an institution or a company of a handful of people, or of hundreds of thousands of people – not as a single, bureaucratic monolith, but as a collection of smaller activities ... each with men and women focusing on a clear and specific objective for that organization ... yet subscribing to the vision, the values and the goals of the overall enterprise.

"I believe strongly that the successful enterprise is one in which every person is challenged to get involved ... to take personal responsibility ... to make a difference ... to act as if the business belongs to each of them.

"As you start your new career, my best advice is to spend the time and energy to really learn about and understand your company or institution ... its history ... its products and services ... its customers ... its competitors.

"Look beyond your immediate assignment as well. Try to empathize with the leaders of your firm. Understand the key issues they are grappling with, and then focus your energy and your activities on helping solve those bigger issues.

"Don't get swept up in the politics of the moment, and don't get stuck in the status quo. Inertia is a powerful force, but you can make it work for you to keep things moving ahead rather than against you to keep things where they've always been.

"Try to get yourself a mentor or two ... people whose judgment you respect and who will give you the benefit of their wisdom.

"And, then, listen. The ability to listen may well be the one skill most critical to your own success.

"Listen to your mentors. Listen to your peers. Listen to the people you work for. Listen to the people working for you. Listen to everyone you can learn from.

"Teamwork is important, too, because your ability to accomplish things by yourself is finite. You can multiply your effectiveness through teamwork.

"And that raises the all-important question of personal leadership. I don't believe there's any single, easy method for being a successful leader. Each of you will have to discover your own leadership talents, develop them, and build on them.

"Keep some balance in your life. You need some time for yourself. Your family and friends need your time and attention as much as your firm does. Family and friends can make your own life more meaningful and productive.

"Finally, there is one absolutely essential ingredient for success, and that's integrity in everything you do.

"I offer these ideas because they have relevance to me, and I believe they can be useful to you, as well.

"To close on this very special day, I'd like to propose an old Irish toast to you. A few years ago, a friend of mine, Charlie Pistor, sent me a copy of a commencement speech he'd given. He'd quoted this saying. I liked it so much, I saved it, and I'd like to share it with you.

"These things I warmly wish for you: someone to love, some work to do, a bit of sun, a bit of cheer, and a guardian angel always near."

"Thank you, and the best of luck to each of you."

Other Thoughts:

"I think of it (Rockwell) as a series of medium-sized businesses, each with very strong management teams with a clear view of where they are going.

"I like to think of an entrepreneur not as a lone wolf starting a small business, but as someone who works for Rockwell: a manager, a supervisor or an engineer."

"We have formed operations to 'de-bureaucratize' this company – to operate with speed and simplicity."

— Donald R. Beall, chairman & CEO

examples. The Rockwell Science Center hosted the centers of excellence for processes such as modeling/simulation, open systems architecture, and software design processes.

A second and complementary technique was to set up corporate technology panels, populated by the corporation's key technologists, in the science and technology disciplines necessary to support business core competencies. These panels, funded by corporate resources, met periodically (in most cases at leading university laboratories) to keep abreast of the worldwide state-of-the-art, and to share expertise corporate wide. Examples were digital signal processing, computational fluid dynamics, computational electromagnetics, and control theory.

C. New Rules for Design-and-Build

A significant and important business/enterprise trend during the late '80s and the '90s was the convergence of engineering processes and manufacturing processes. Traditionally, the manufacturing process accommodated unconstrained engineering inputs (build to print). However, new process technologies in both disciplines (engineering and manufacturing) forced a "mutual accommodation" – a necessary compatibility between design rules and manufacturing rules.

This evolution was initially recognized in the early development of semiconductor design and manufacturing processes. The trend continued in the higher level of electronics inter-connects in printed circuit boards, in the design and manufacture of composite structures, in the design and manufacture of aero structures using integrated computational fluid dynamics/computational electromagnetic techniques, etc. This convergence required concurrent and/or coordinated development of engineering and manufacturing processes; and introduced manufacturing "yield-driven" metrics, such as six sigma, which led to higher quality levels and lower cost.

Rockwell management was at the very forefront of this transition, and organizational align-ments and management processes were implemented to provide effective and disciplined interaction between engineering and manufacturing. To facilitate this interaction, Rockwell developed a joint engineering/manufacturing management education program. This initiative was an inter-business unit, case study program that promoted innovative solutions to the particular challenges facing Rockwell business units.

D. Managing Domain Knowledge

Rockwell management understood that the increasing rate of technological innovation was resulting in a similarly increasing proportion of a company's value being represented by the value of knowledge —"soft" capital vs. "hard" capital. This, in turn, required increasing emphasis on the management of intellectual property — patents, copyrights, trade secrets, proprietary market knowledge (domain expertise), etc. The Rockwell Management Process Task Force addressed this phenomenon with local and corporate seminars to promote awareness and understanding of the complex value structures. Management processes were implemented to deal with related metrics and control, which included patent/copyright management, controlled knowledge sharing with the supply chain and/or external teammates, information privacy control, etc.

E. Rockwell University

As a further step to obtain the "buy-in" and commitment of all senior managers to the values and vision for the company, a Rockwell Executive Management School was estab-lished. The school also brought in leading-edge management thinkers to stimulate the organization for higher performance and marketplace innovation (e.g., Gary Hamel, Jim Collins, C.K. Prahalad, Peter Drucker). Each school session ran for a full week and was

23. Rockwell's Engineer of the Year Award recognized the company's engineers and scientists for significant technical achievement.

Leadership Assessment

	Never 1	Seldom 2	Sometimes 3	Usually 4	Always 5
Vision and Ownership					
Reinforces the Rockwell vision and strategic business imperatives					
Creates an expectation of success and inspires others to commitment					
Communicates business challenges in a positive manner					
Accepts responsibility for failures and successes					
Establishes meaningful objectives to achieve success					
Passion/Energy					
Seeks new ways to continuously improve the work environment					
Pitches in as an active team member					
Responds quickly to customers, management and/or employee needs					
Develops multiple options and is persevering					
Accountability					
Is willing to make unpopular decisions					
Accepts responsibility for own decisions and those of subordinates					
Excellence					
Achieved results add value to the organization					
Selects the most important areas to work on from a range of competing priorities					
Identifies and offers realistic solutions to problems					
Sets challenging standards and expectations for outstanding performance					
Leads by example; personally models the best practices					
Empowerment/Involvement					
Shares credit, recognition and visibility with others					
Shows appreciation for contributions and achievements					
Empowers employees and gives commensurate authority					
Strikes balance between freedom of action and abandonment					
Teamwork					
Actively contributes to and supports multi-organizational efforts					
Respects the talent and contributions of all team members; helps to create an environment where everyone feels able to participate					
Values diversity as a strength to the organization					
Receptivity to Change					
Handles crisis and unexpected events effectively					
Anticipates changing requirements and prepares for them					
Persuasively and clearly communicates new ideas; builds ownership for new approaches					
Adapts quickly to new initiatives					
Development					
Gives frequent, candid feedback on performance and career development					
Selects/hires talented people; frees them up for training and development					
Recognizes and rewards individual and team achievements					
Integrity					
Creates/supports a compliance culture; reinforces compliance requirements					
Encourages team members to raise compliance/integrity concerns					
Adheres to highest standards of business ethics ... does the "right thing"					
Actions consistent with words ... "walks the talk"					
Delivers on commitments to suppliers, customers, and/or employees					

Leadership Specification
(Senior Executive Succession/Development)

- Vision ... Ability to stimulate the business organization to look ahead and shape the future
- Exemplifies Rockwell's leadership attitudes (per Vision)
- Passionate and relentless about gaining a sustainable global competitive advantage
- Conceptual thinker ... ability to deal with the abstract
- Good balance of leadership skills – hands-on/hands-off
- Sets high expectations ... stretch targets ... holds accountable
- Ownership ... always is focused on what's right for the business
- Inspires team to become enthusiastic and engaged
- Strong people orientation ... brings out the best in people ... selects well ... deals with non-performers
- High energy level ... pro-active ... a sense of urgency
- Broad experience ...
- Domestic and international
- Multi-functional
- Exposure to several businesses
- Business turnaround/start-up experience
- Business process understanding
- Strong marketing and customer skills
- Maturity, judgment and ability to go it alone
- Communication skills ... verbal and written
- Integrity ... ethics beyond reproach
- Flexibility ... quick to adapt to change ... experiments ... innovative
- Team player
- Competitive spirit ... focus on being the best

PROVEN ACHIEVER WHO GETS RESULTS

Note: These skills and attributes need to be matched on a case-by-case basis to the needs of the business.

opened and closed by either the chairman or chief operating officer. The closing sessions were most helpful as they gave a "no holds barred" opportunity for the managers to tell the chairman or COO as to how they saw things and what needed to be done … all focused on Team Rockwell not "we versus they."

F. Engineer of the Year Awards – Celebrating Innovation

An important ingredient in "innovation" is a workplace environment that motivates and sustains the process of innovation. A couple of important factors that helped provide such an environment at Rockwell included corporate recognition of key technological innovation successes.

Recognition is a great motivator for follow-on innovation in a total technical community. Rockwell invented and implemented the corporate "Engineer of the Year" program that recognized engineers and scientists for significant technical achievement. Sub-elements of the program were implemented within many of Rockwell's business units. The highly visible corporate wide (and public) recognition, along with the clear and sincere support shown by all levels of management, provided excellent motivation for technical excellence across the company. The chairman and the top operating management recognized the value of this Engineer of the Year program and were personally involved in the award ceremonies.

Also, in the late '80s and early '90s, in published results of technical university assessments, Rockwell was identified as one of the top five companies in the U.S. for engineers to work. This helped considerably in recruiting top graduates who could provide real innovative leverage within the company. The Engineer of the Year program weighed significantly in forming assessment results.

Independent Proactive Board

During the "evolutionary" years Rockwell had an increasingly strong and independent board and always was a leader in very disciplined corporate governance practices.

Rockwell's board of directors also played a key role in shaping the strategies, goals and objectives for the corporation and supporting the senior management team in achievement of those goals. Senior operating management, even though not directors, participated in all board meetings to gain corporate experience and enhance their development.

Leadership specifications – skills, attributes, values and experiences – were identified and discussed with the board as a way to screen future leaders.

Annual company goals and objectives for every business and the total company were reviewed with the board, and executive compensation and stock rewards were granted against achievement of goals and objectives. All major commitments such as mergers, joint ventures and acquisitions as well as major internal investments in capital and R&D were, of course, reviewed with the board. Non-financial goals also were assessed, for example, how Rockwell was perceived with respect to diversity initiatives, protecting the environment, and being a good neighbor to and partner with the community. Executive compensation was always performance-based and conservative – particularly related to today's practices.

Rockwell Vision

Be THE BEST Diversified High Technology Company
in the World

AS JUDGED BY

Customers:	Be The Supplier of Choice
Employees:	Be recognized as The Best Place to work
Shareowners:	Provide Highest Industry Returns to our Investors
Community:	Be recognized as Engaged, Enthusiastic Supporters of our communities

ACTION STRATEGIES

Create the World's Most Successful Customers

- Continuously create new customer value
- Always strive to exceed customer expectations
- Be the most customer responsive company in the world
- Establish win-win relationships with our customers and suppliers
- Provide quality, delivery and service second to none

Aggressively Pursue Global Growth

- Lead through innovation and the application of advanced technologies
- Work together and share resources across the company
- Acquire or team with leading companies to enhance competitiveness
- Make our core processes the best in the world
- Continuously grow worldwide market share in each business

Execute Leading Edge Practices

- Continuously measure and improve all that we do
- Recognize and reward based on individual and team performance
- Benchmark and implement the best ways of doing business
- Commit to continuous learning and development
- Empower multifunctional teams
- Ensure best informed employees
- Seek out and nurture new ideas from everyone
- Align functional policies and procedures to support our vision

Contribute to the Well-Being of Our Communities

- Engage in civic activities as informed and involved citizens
- Volunteer for health, business, social and youth activities
- Support charitable and cultural organizations
- Take part in educational activities, including school boards, planning committees and mentoring
- Preserve, protect and improve our environment

ATTITUDES

- Unquestioned integrity
- Strong preference for action and a passion to win
- Excited, energized and engaged
- Zeal for continuous learning
- Commitment to being a team player
- Diversity valued as strength
- Listening is as important as talking
- Each of us is responsible for making this Vision real and living it every day
- Deep-seated respect for the individual

THE ROCKWELL CREDO:
WHAT WE BELIEVE

We believe maximizing the satisfaction of our customers is our most important concern as a means of warranting their continued loyalty.

We believe in providing superior value to customers through high-quality, technologically advanced, fairly priced products and customer service designed to meet customer needs better than all alternatives.

We believe Rockwell people are our most important assets, making the critical difference in how well Rockwell performs; and, through their work and effort, separating Rockwell from all competitors.

We believe we have an obligation for the well-being of the communities in which we live and work.

We believe excellence is the standard for all we do, achieved by encouraging and nourishing:

• Respect for the individual

• Honest, open communication

• Individual development and satisfaction

• A sense of ownership and responsibility for Rockwell's success

• Participation, cooperation and teamwork

• Creativity, innovation and initiative

• Prudent risk-taking

• Recognition and rewards for achievement

We believe success is realized by:

• Achieving leadership in the markets we serve

• Focusing our resources and energy on global markets where our technology, knowledge, capabilities and understanding of customers combine to provide the opportunity for leadership

• Maintain the highest standard of ethics and integrity in every action we take, in everything we do

We believe the ultimate measure of our success is the ability to provide a superior value to our shareowners, balancing near-term and long-term objectives to achieve both a competitive return on investment and consistent increased market value.

A FINANCIAL OVERVIEW
OF THE EVOLUTION YEARS

The following financial overview describes the change in composition and increasing market focus that occurred prior to the major strategic moves to separate the company into several very focused public companies.

All of the following charts show financial information up to the sale of the aerospace business to Boeing.

Chart 1 Sales by Business 1968-1995

$ in Millions

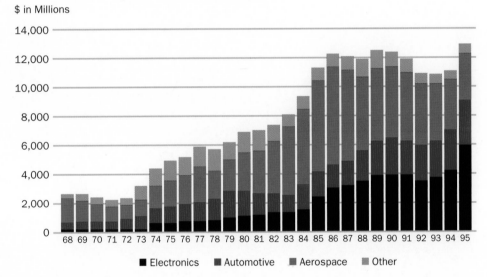

Chart 1 illustrates clearly the changing composition of sales among the Aerospace, Electronics, Automotive, and other businesses. Total company sales grew from just over $2 billion in 1968 to over $12 billion in the mid-'80s. One can see the tremendous growth of the Aerospace business up until 1986. Aerospace sales peaked in 1986 at almost $7 billion and declined to just over $3 billion before the sale to Boeing in 1996. Electronics grew steadily throughout the period. Automotive sales grew to about $3 billion prior to its spin-off. The "other businesses" (shown in light blue) were significant contributors and were all divested by 1995.

Because so much of Rockwell's aerospace growth related to a few mega-programs with limited life (e.g., Space Shuttle, B-1B bomber, GPS satellites), it was clear that new growth vehicles were necessary – hence; the major focus on creating a major and growing position in selected high-growth electronics businesses – more on that later.

Chart 2 **Operating Income by Business 1968-1995**

$ in Millions

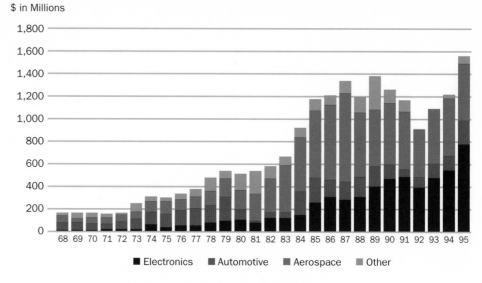

■ Electronics   ■ Automotive   ■ Aerospace   ■ Other

Chart 3 **Cash Flow by Business 1968-1995**

$ in Millions

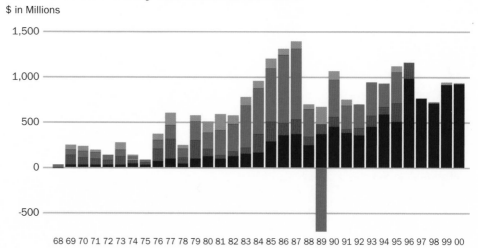

■ Electronics   ■ Automotive   ■ Aerospace   ■ Other

NOTE: 1988 was the effect of a large tax payment upon completion of the multi-year B-1 Bomber production contract.

Chart 4 **Capital Expenditures 1968-1995**

$ in Millions

Total $10 Billion

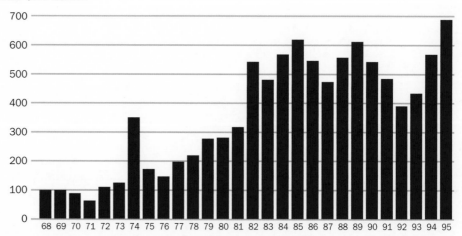

Chart 5 **Company Funded R&D 1968-1995**
$ in Millions

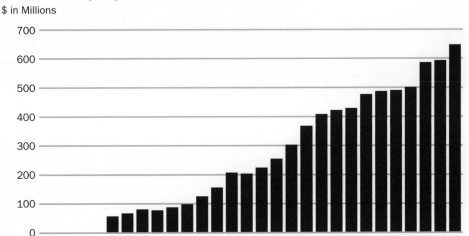

Chart 6 **Share Repurchase**
$ in Millions
Total $5.1 Billion

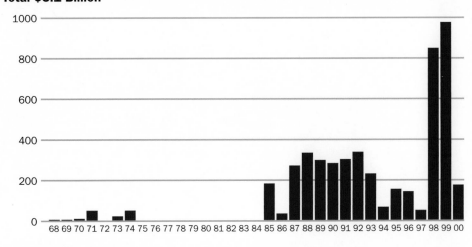

Additional perspective on those transformation years is provided by reviewing the composition of Operating Income and Cash Flow (Charts 2 and 3), CAPEX (Chart 4), R&D (Chart 5), and Share Repurchases (Chart 6).

The tremendous contribution of the Aerospace business to income and cash is very evident. Those resources and the proceeds from the ultimate sale of the "other businesses" were crucial to the development of the major growth vehicle – Electronics. All of Rockwell's businesses benefited from steady and very substantial R&D and CAPEX investments. Performance was so favorable that cash also was available for a major recapitalization of the company through stock repurchase. In fact, the repurchases reduced the outstanding shares by over 30 percent.

Another important fact not shown on the charts is that Rockwell's market value grew steadily to about $14 billion at the end of the FY '97 (including the value of the Boeing shares received in December '96 on completion of the sale of the Aerospace businesses).

AN OVERVIEW OF THE TRANSFORMATION STORY

24. B-1A – A B-1A test flight aircraft shows its sleek platform. The original contract for 244 B-1A Strategic Bombers was cancelled by President Carter on June 30, 1977. Fortunately, the B-1B program was resurrected by President Reagan in 1981. (USAF photo)

Now, we are going to review the activities of each of the primary businesses of Rockwell – significant events that occurred in the '70s and '80s; and strategic actions under way at each business in the '90s prior to the Boeing transaction.

In addition to the following descriptions about each business, a wealth of information, terrific resource material, analyst presentations, SEC materials, etc. are available at each of these business's websites.

AEROSPACE

During the first few years after the 1967 merger, Aerospace sales declined with the completion of the production phase of the Apollo and Saturn programs, although missions continued through 1975 (Apollo-Soyuz/Skylab). Various defense electronics programs also were in a decline. However, in the early 1970s, Rockwell won the B-1 bomber development program and, very importantly, the Space Shuttle vehicle also was awarded to Rockwell. Another significant win was the Space Shuttle Main Engine contract (these are the three reusable liquid oxygen/liquid hydrogen engines that are part of the Space Shuttle vehicle). The Martin Company won the External Tank contract and Thiokol won the Solid Reusable Booster program. Rockwell also was awarded the role as the integrating contractor of the entire system for NASA. These two massive programs were the primary growth drivers of the company through 1986 when Aerospace sales peaked at almost $7 billion. The one reduction (Chart 7) from 1977 to 1978 was caused by the cancellation of the B-1 program by President Carter. The program (B-1B) was restarted by President Reagan in 1981.

Chart 7 shows Aerospace sales up to the point of the 1996 Boeing transaction.

Chart 7 **Aerospace Sales**

$ in Millions

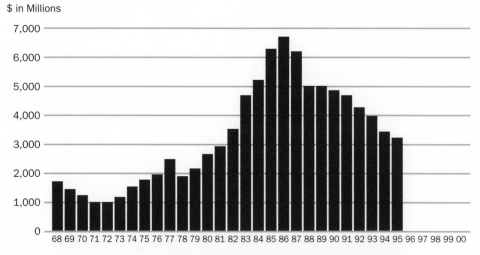

25

26

27

During this period the company also was awarded and built the multiple satellites required for the Global Positioning System (GPS) constellation and several classified satellite programs.

Rockwell captured the original GPS contract in 1974 and launched the first Block I GPS satellite in February 1978. The company went on to produce the Block II and IIA at its Seal Beach, Calif. facility, many of which function well beyond their expected service life. Boeing is now building the next-generation GPS IIF satellites in El Segundo, Calif. Designed as a military navigation and time-keeping satellite, today GPS is applied in thousands of commercial and consumer applications.

The defense electronics business won all of the flight control, inertial navigation and flight computers for the Minuteman III and MX Peacekeeper ICBM systems. Rocketdyne produced the fourth stage for Peacekeeper that featured a re-startable liquid-fueled engine that increased system accuracy. The liquid-fuel stage was unique in the fact that it could be stored for long periods in underground silos on the Peacekeeper, which consisted of three other solid fuel stages.

Significant work also was conducted for the U.S. Navy submarine programs, under which Rockwell built all of the navigators for the nuclear fleet. Initial work for the Navy began in 1958 when the Autonetics N6 autonavigator was selected for use on the Nautilus, the nation's first nuclear powered submarine. The N6 guided the first undersea transit of the North Pole. An improved N6 was subsequently selected for the Polaris ballistic missile submarine fleet. The company was recognized for developing a navigation system that did not require the submarine to surface to take a stellar sighting fix, thus reducing vulnerability to attack. Autonetics next developed the enhanced N7 (Navy designation, Mk2 SINS [Submarine Inertial Navigation System]) that was deployed on the George Washington class boats. The Mk2 Mod 7 SINS is currently operating aboard the Ohio class Trident ballistic missile submarines.

In addition, significant work was accomplished in Ships Control Stations for the submarine fleet, as well as very important sonar signal processing systems. The company also developed and produced very large quantities of the Hellfire anti-tank weapon system and the GBU-15 guided bomb system, a predecessor of today's precision-guided weapons.

The company invested heavily in the various Strategic Defense Initiative (SDI) technologies and won many important missile defense development contracts. Important research contracts also were won in advanced aircraft concepts, such as the futuristic HiMAT (Highly Maneuverable Aircraft Technology) RPRV (Remotely Piloted Research Vehicle), the precursor to today's UAVs. Rockwell also designed and built the first international X-Plane, the X-31A EFM (Enhanced Fighter Maneuverability) aircraft. X-31A explored unique high-alpha flight testing and was later resurrected by Boeing as the X-31A VECTOR for the U.S. Navy. In the

25. Global Positioning System Block II. The first Rockwell-developed USAF GPS Block I satellite was launched on February 22, 1978. Unknown at the time was the tremendous impact that GPS would have on the civilian world. *(Photo/Illustration by Erik Simonsen)*

26. A Minuteman III ICBM launches from its underground silo at Vandenberg AFB, Calif. Rockwell developed the original guidance system for the Boeing-built ICBM. *(USAF photo)*

27. Autonetics developed the enhanced N6 unit designated Mk2 Submarine Inertial Navigation System for the George Washington class nuclear submarines. *(U.S. Navy photo)*

28   29   30   3

28. HELLFIRE – Originally developed and built at its Duluth, Georgia, facility, the extremely successful air or ground-launched Rockwell Hellfire missile has continued its longevity under other contractors. Photo depicts a Hellfire air-to-ground missile being launched from a U.S. Army AH-64 Apache. Hellfire also is the primary weapon of the USAF Predator and Reaper Unmanned Aerial Vehicles (UAVs). *(U.S. Army photo)*

29. X-31A EFM – The Rockwell X-31A EFM (Enhanced Fighter Maneuverability) was the first international X-Plane. Using a unique vectored thrust paddle system, the X-31A explored controlled flight at high-angle-of-attack. Continuing its valuable research career, the X-31A recently was brought back into service in the Boeing/U.S. Navy VECTOR program. *(NASA photo)*

30. Space Shuttle – Another spectacular liftoff of the Space Shuttle from the Kennedy Space Center. The Shuttle continues to carry vital segments to the International Space Station. *(NASA photo)*

31. Space Shuttle and X-40A – Rare photo of the Space Shuttle and the unmanned autonomous X-40A Space Maneuver Vehicle (SMV) together on the tarmac at Dryden Flight Research Center. *(NASA photo)*

area of hypersonic airframe design and propulsion, Rockwell was the lead contractor for the X-30 National Aerospace Plane (NASP) team.

The company was the prime contractor for the AC-130U Gunship program that has seen significant deployment in Iraq and Afghanistan. The AC-130U offered vast improvements over the older AC-130H Gunship, including a new weapons digital fire-control radar, all-light-level television and expanded precision weapons capability. Incidentally, the B-1B Lancer bomber has delivered more precision guided ordnance in Iraq than any other aircraft by a large margin.

The company performed very significant aerostructures support to Boeing on the 747 and 757 programs. Also won were significant contracts for the operational support of the Space Shuttle and for major elements of the International Space Station. In addition, Rockwell conducted significant work on missile defense technology, including kinetic kill vehicles, and on airborne laser weapons systems.

Leadership programs and technologies also existed in the energy area. The company had done early work in the nuclear field…space-borne nuclear power sources and was a leader in the early work on fast breeder reactors. The Department of Energy (DOE) contracted with Rockwell to build the steam generators, using proprietary liquid sodium (the heat transfer material) technology for the Clinch River demonstration program. Unfortunately, the country did not go forward with this work. Much work was also done in coal lique-faction and gasification. The company also managed the Hanford and Rocky Flats nuclear weapon facilities for the DOE.

Even before one knew of the collapse of the former Soviet Union, it was clear that Rockwell's Aerospace business would decline from its mid-1980s peak. During the period of the early to mid-1990s, major consolidation was occurring in the aerospace industry, leading to a few major surviving aerospace companies: Boeing (of course to include Rockwell's Aerospace business, McDonnell Douglas and large parts of Hughes aircraft), Lockheed Martin, Northrop Grumman, and Raytheon. Scale is important in the major systems aerospace business. Rockwell could have chosen to participate in the consolidation as one of the survivors.

All during this period, a small group of the top team continually examined strategic options available to the company. That team in the mid-90s included Don Beall, Don Davis, Mike Barnes, Charlie Harff, Lee Cramer, Bill Calise, Morgan Stanley, Chadbourne (Rockwell's corporate attorneys), UBS-Warburg (the previous Dillon-Read, long time investment advisors), and Deloitte and Touche. Many others were involved in various considered alternatives, of course. Appendix 1 entitled, "The Leaders" includes additional very key people involved throughout this historic transformation of Rockwell.

It should be noted that this was a period when overall results were essentially flat for several years, masking the tremendous growth occurring in the Electronics businesses. Earnings overall were steadily improving, helped importantly by the continued recapitalization (major stock repurchase made possible by the strong cash generation from Aerospace). There was clear evidence that the overall company was undervalued in the market. It also was believed that all of the businesses operated with leadership management practices and could operate as separate companies, should that path be chosen.

Many alternatives were considered for many years, leading to the difficult decision to sell the Aerospace business to Boeing. Once that choice was made, it was a foregone conclusion that the Automotive business should be spun off as a separate company, leaving the continuing Rockwell as a strong diversified electronics company.

32

B-1B Strategic Bomber

President Reagan announced on October 2, 1981 that as part of his Strategic Modernization Program, 100 B-1Bs and 132 Advanced Technology Bombers, later designated the B-2, would be built. A determined Rockwell leader, Sam Iacobellis (dubbed "Mr. B-1B"), and his team kept the $20.5 billion program on track. Not long after the contract award, four and sometimes five of the sleek bombers were rolling out the door every month at the Rockwell Palmdale facility. To put that in perspective – the total parts for the assembly of a single B-1 is equivalent to 15 F-16 fighters. The 100th B-1B rolled out of the factory on January 20, 1988. This achievement is especially significant because the B-1 program was a fixed price contract with very stringent requirements. Despite those requirements, all 100 B-1Bs were built and delivered ahead of schedule and below budget. This certainly was one of the best-managed large Department of Defense contracts ever. It also was a great contributor to the profits and cash flow of Rockwell.

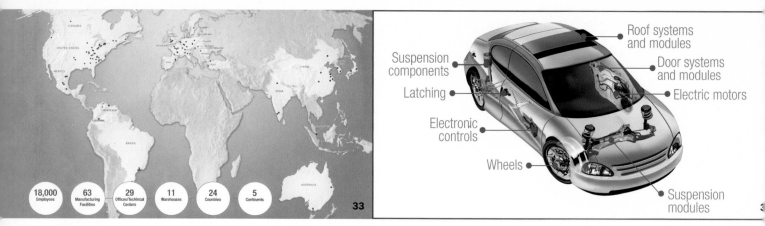

AUTOMOTIVE

Chart 8 shows the sales of Rockwell's Automotive businesses up until the time of its spin-off in 1997, as Meritor, Inc. At that time, sales were just over $3 billion.

The Automotive business of Rockwell was comprised of two very different businesses: Commercial Vehicle Systems (CVS) and Light Vehicle Systems (LVS). Both, of course, are cyclical businesses.

The CVS business has leading market share positions in its primary product lines in North America. Major products are single and tandem rear axles, front axles, braking systems and foundation air brakes, suspensions systems and ride control products – all supplied to medium- and heavy-duty trucks and specialty vehicle OEMs. Outside of the U.S., most heavy truck and other commercial vehicle producers historically have been vertically integrated in their drivetrain components (axles, drivelines and transmissions). CVS was successful in Europe in de-integrating Fiat, Unic, Magirus Deutsch, Volvo, and some others. In other countries, many joint ventures were launched in order to participate in local markets, e.g., India, Brazil, China, Mexico, Venezuela, Argentina, Europe, etc. In short, CVS became an important global player … albeit in a cyclical business that was very profitable in the up cycles and manageable in the down period.

The Light Vehicle Systems products business of Rockwell was formed largely around acquired companies and included many products — wheels, springs, suspension components (e.g., stabilizer bars and struts), plastic subassemblies and parts, sunroofs, latches (for doors, trunks, hoods, etc.), window regulators (including motors), etc. It became a major strategic objective

Chart 8 Automotive Sales 1968-1996

$ in Millions

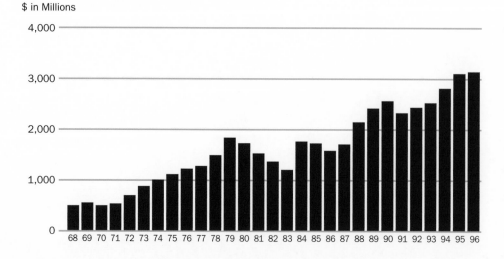

35. Commercial Vehicle Systems automated axle gear-cutting process

36. Fumagalli superspoke steel wheel

to work with the OEMs to earn a position as a systems supplier (for example … the supply to Volkswagen of a complete sunroof system that could be inserted in their assembly line … or supplying a complete door system that could be inserted in the assembly line that included latches, window regulators, motors, etc.). Over the years, the business developed a significant presence in every major market around the world. The Light Vehicle business was viewed as a major growth opportunity through the '90s and at the time the entire automotive business was spun-out as Meritor Automotive in 1997.

The Automotive businesses had grown to about $3 billion in sales prior to the spin in 1997. The business was profitable, with positive cash flow. Commercial Vehicle Systems represented about two-thirds of the business at that time.

ELECTRONICS

Electronics businesses have become the primary creators of shareowner value for the Rockwell shareowners. However, remember that much of that was made possible by the tremendous performance of the Aerospace businesses with the related cash flow and profitability, and through the sale of the "other" businesses.

The growth of the Electronics businesses within Rockwell was made possible by a combination of major acquisitions, internal business development, sharing of internal capabilities developed for other purposes and the contribution of the Rockwell Science Center … a major repository of leadership technologies in software, control theory, electronic materials (e.g. silicon and gallium arsenide), as well as basic mathematics, chemistry, physics, etc.

In the broadest sense, what was to become Rockwell Electronics was the result of the 1971 investment in Collins Radio Company and its subsequent acquisition in 1973; the acquisition of the Allen-Bradley Company in 1985; and the internal development of the Rockwell Semiconductor business.

There are several important chapters:

First, look at the growth of Electronics Sales (Chart 9 below) within Rockwell prior to the subsequent spin-offs.

The Electronics Sales chart (Chart 9) shows clearly the important contribution of Collins, Automation and Semiconductors to the growth of the Electronics segment within Rockwell. The dip in the early 1990s is due to the Collins' sale of certain commercial telecom product lines to the French company, Alcatel. Collins had been a niche player in the microwave transmission business for many years and decided to redeploy those assets to its stronger segments in avionics and government telecommunication served markets.

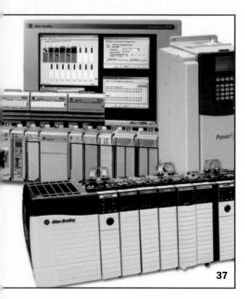

37. In 1999, Rockwell Automation introduced the Logix control platform which has had a revolutionary impact on manufacturing. Logix gives manufacturers the ability to integrate multiple control disciplines, such as discrete, motion, batch and continuous process, motor, and safety, on a single platform – providing the foundation for a single plant-wide automation system.

AUTOMATION

In 1985, Rockwell acquired the Allen-Bradley Company, headquartered in Milwaukee. The business was privately held by a trust, the beneficiaries of which were the heirs of the company's founders. The company had grown from a supplier of electrical control products (relays, motor controllers and drives, switches, passive components, etc.) to a broad-based supplier of very sophisticated computer-controlled factory automation control and communication systems. Rockwell surprised the world's largest factory automation company, Siemens of Germany, by out-bidding them in a deal worth about $1.6 billion in cash.

Rockwell acquired Allen-Bradley with the strategic intent of becoming a leading global participant in the high growth automation markets. Allen-Bradley had excellent management and clearly was the North American leader in its served markets. Its international presence was limited and represented a great opportunity. Rockwell decided to forego short-term profitability for long-term growth and encouraged Allen-Bradley to invest heavily for growth. Many smaller companies were acquired to provide market-extension and/or product growth. In 1994, Rockwell acquired Reliance Electric for $1.1 billion in cash to bolster Allen-Bradley's electric motor and drives business. Reliance also had a major business in mechanical power transfer products. All through the 1980s and 1990s, major investments were made in new systems and products, often aided by the technology and people of other Rockwell businesses and, very importantly, the Rockwell Science Center capabilities.

Chart 9 shows the importance of the Automation business to the growth of Rockwell's Electronics segment.

Chart 9 **Electronic Sales by Business 1968-2000**

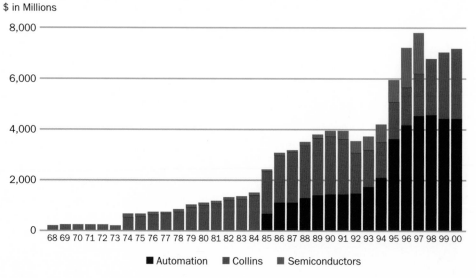

$ in Millions

Automation   Collins   Semiconductors

SEMICONDUCTOR BUSINESS

The history of the semiconductor business of Rockwell is unique, in that it was established and grown organically (rather than through acquisitions) from several distinct sources within the company. The three organizations that played the largest roles were Autonetics, Collins, and the Science Center.

During the time that Autonetics (the electronics capability of North American) was developing the flight control, navigation, and computers for the nation's ICBMs and submarines, it had to know enough about the early world of integrated circuits such that it could specify its requirements to manufacturers (e.g., Texas Instruments). In that process, the research laboratories of

Autonetics as well as the Rockwell Science Center developed "pilot-line" capabilities in the most advanced semiconductor design and processing technologies of that time. Autonetics also had developed many advanced capabilities in signal processing electronics and related communications technologies. These two early capabilities – semiconductor processing/design and communications signal processing – formed the basis (now termed the "core competencies") of what would later become the Rockwell Semiconductor business.

In 1968, the North American Rockwell Microelectronics Company was created to target some of the emerging commercial applications of these foundation capabilities. The initial semiconductor products were manufactured in a process called PMOS (for P-channel Metal Oxide Semiconductor), the precursor to today's ubiquitous CMOS (for Complementary Metal Oxide Semiconductor) technology. An initial market application was calculator circuits for the Sharp company of Japan, which turned out to be a major business success and was the foundation for a business partnership between Sharp and the Rockwell businesses that continues to this day. But what would turn out to be the real home run for this new business was the development of the first facsimile modems using large-scale integrated circuits (which used both of the core competencies: communications signal processing and semiconductor device design). It was the worldwide success of facsimile machines (again with Japanese customer-partners) and the majority semiconductor market share that Rockwell built and maintained in this product space that propelled what would become Rockwell Semiconductor Systems and, later, Conexant.

When Collins Radio Company was acquired, it brought a wealth of additional semiconductor and communications capabilities that were integrated over time with the Rockwell semiconductor initiative.

In particular, the Collins team brought deep understanding of radio frequency (RF) communications, as well as RF semiconductor circuit design. This RF expertise would later be mated with the capabilities of the Rockwell Science Center in high performance gallium arsenide semiconductor devices to develop products for wireless communications applications.

The greatest success that resulted from this combination was the early use of gallium arsenide devices for the power amplification function in mobile phones. Rockwell Semiconductor Systems and then Conexant became a leader in this application and, today, Skyworks (created by a spin-off from Conexant) holds the number one market position for cellular power amplifiers with shipments of approximately 500 million units annually.

It was in the mid-1980s that the business success of the Rockwell semiconductor initiatives accelerated, and the company increased its focus on the commercial semiconductor opportunity. The first driver for this was the previously mentioned facsimile application. By this time, facsimile machines had declined in price substantially (largely as a result of the cost savings of large scale integrated circuit chipsets) and the transmission speed and image quality had improved dramatically. Every business decided fax machines were essential, and Rockwell had a 70 percent worldwide market share and a very high growth business.

What would later prove to be even more successful was the retargeting of the facsimile technology to sending data between computers over telephone lines. This was called a "data modem" and, with the amazing growth of the Personal Computer (late-'80s) and then the Internet (mid-'90s), it became a huge growth market. The Rockwell semiconductor business built and held the top market share position in the data modem space through several product generations (higher and higher speeds).

In total, the semiconductor business' facsimile and data modem revenue grew almost tenfold from approximately $150 million in the late-'80s to more than $1.5 billion by the mid-'90s. With this rapid growth, Rockwell increased its investments in the semiconductor business

38. Rockwell chipsets are used in a variety of wireless communications products worldwide, including cellular phones. The global wireless market allows people the freedom to communicate anytime, anywhere.

39. The first communication from a man on the lunar surface to Earth, including the first television pictures, were transmitted and received by Collins communications equipment

40. Handheld Defense Advanced GPS Receiver (DAGR)

significantly, primarily for increased manufacturing capacity and advanced process capabilities as well as for acquisitions designed to broaden the unit's addressed markets.

By 1998, the Rockwell Semiconductor Systems business was a material component of the overall company, but with a capital investment and marketplace volatility profile very different from the remaining business units. This divergence led to the 1998 decision to establish Conexant as a public company owned by the Rockwell shareowners.

COLLINS

The Collins Radio Company was experiencing major financial problems in the late 1960s. This was caused by a weak period in the commercial airline business, a prime market for Collins. At the same time, a fall-off in defense spending was occurring and, even more importantly for Collins, major investments were being made in radical new systems to capitalize on the move to digital transmission and switching – a new field for Collins. Collins was a very strong player in avionics for commercial aviation, commercial telecommunications (analog microwave radios and multiplex for telephony), and various government telecommunications requirements. In the government arena, Collins was a major supplier and innovator in all forms and frequency ranges of communications requirements. Examples: Collins was the major supplier of the communications to the nuclear submarine fleet. Imagine, a C-130 aircraft orbiting with a 5-mile long antenna deployed required to transmit under water a Very Low Frequency (VLF) signal, highly encrypted that was the only way of reliably relaying the President's decision to the nuclear subs! Collins provided all of that capability.

Collins also provided the ability to communicate with the Apollo spacecraft from Earth, and provided the secure communications for tactical and strategic aircraft. Secure communications to the ICBM commanders also was provided by Collins. The ground stations (large antennas with associated electronics) for commercial and military communications were a Collins capability. Commercial telephony transmission capabilities for countries like Korea, Mexico, Saudi Arabia, Iran, Egypt, Algeria, and the U.S. were provided by Collins. Collins was (and is) a leading supplier of avionics systems to the commercial and general aviation aircraft around the world. Collins also is the major supplier of GPS user equipment for military use...everything from the handset carried by the soldier on the ground to the navigators employed in precision-guided weapons. Air Force One and the entire strategic aircraft capability of the United States rely on Collins satellite and other communications systems.

Rockwell invested in Collins in 1971 and acquired the company in 1973. Beall led the investment team and joined Collins at the time of the investment and was subsequently named president of Collins after the acquisition. Collins' contribution to the growth of Rockwell's Electronics segment is shown clearly in Chart 9.

THE TRANSFORMED ROCKWELL

As discussed earlier, in 1996 the aerospace business was sold to Boeing. Then, in 1997 the Automotive business was spun off as a new public company—Meritor.

That left Rockwell as a focused diversified electronics company serving avionics and communications (Collins), automation and semiconductor markets.

Don Davis became the CEO of Rockwell in the fall of 1997; Beall remained as non-CEO chairman until early 1998 and on the board until 2001. Don (Davis) and his team decided early in 1998 to spin-off the semiconductor business to be completely owned by the Rockwell shareowners—Conexant.

Don and his team recognized that the dynamics of a semiconductor business was very different from Rockwell's automation and avionics businesses, including its markets, products and investment requirements. Semiconductor Systems is a very cyclical business, requiring high demands for capital, long-term sustainable investment and different compensation schemes for its employees. These characteristics, combined with their understanding that there were very few successful semiconductor businesses operating in multi-business companies, drove this difficult decision. More importantly, Semiconductor Systems had excellent people, facilities, financial resources and an exciting array of new products. The company had full confidence in the management team and believed they could unlock greater value for shareowners as a stand-alone business.

Perhaps, the most difficult decision Don and the team made took place in 2001 when it was decided to spin-off Rockwell Collins into a new separately traded, stand-alone company. However, it became clear that the benefits of operating both Rockwell Automation and Rockwell Collins under one corporate roof had diminished over time. In fact, very few synergies existed between the two companies. As stand-alone, world renowned companies with leading market positions, it was believed that each of these leading global businesses would be better able to focus on enhancing its strategic positions, serving its customers and creating value for shareowners. Don and the team also knew that independence would enable each company to allocate its resources, better "incentivize" its employees and pursue strategies that responded to each company's specific needs and market opportunities. Rockwell Collins, like all Rockwell businesses, had a great management team that was capable of creating future value for its shareowners. This has certainly been the case.

BOEING TRANSACTION

The Rockwell aerospace businesses sold to Boeing had sales of about $3 billion in 1996, the year of the transaction. Boeing assumed about $2.3 billion of Rockwell debt and distributed Boeing stock to the Rockwell shareowner worth about $900 million at that time. Thus, the primary consideration was cash. The value to the Rockwell shareowner per share of Rockwell stock of the Boeing stock received is computed at 8.4 percent of the value of the Boeing share price; this has been adjusted for splits. The larger value to the Rockwell shareowner derived from the significant benefit of the debt assumption; those resources were used to further recapitalize Rockwell primarily through substantial additional stock repurchases; Rockwell repurchased stock with a value of about $2.3 billion from 1997 to 2000. Importantly, the transaction was structured to be tax free to the Rockwell shareowner.

More important than that arithmetic was the enormous benefit to Boeing of the Rockwell people and businesses.

Shortly after acquiring the Rockwell aerospace businesses, Boeing acquired the Hughes Space and Communication business, and the McDonnell Douglas Company. In 1996, Boeing's sales were about $23 billion … $17 billion for Commercial Airplanes and about $6 billion of mainly Government sales. For 2006, Boeing sales had grown to about $62 billion of which more than half was from their non-Commercial Airplane business. Thus, the consolidation of the businesses of Rockwell, Hughes, and McDonnell Douglas with Boeing's similar businesses has resulted in a huge and very successful aerospace enterprise.

Rockwell can be especially proud of the performance within Boeing of the Rockwell people and businesses transferred. For example, Jim Albaugh is president and CEO of Boeing Integrated Defense Systems (this business today is over $32 billion in revenue and includes all of the non-commercial airplane businesses of Boeing). James Bell is a corporate executive vice president and chief financial officer (he served as interim CEO during the transitional period before Jim McNerney became chairman and CEO). Rick Stephens is a corporate senior vice president (SVP) in charge of Human Resources and Administration. Shephard Hill is president of Boeing International. Howard Chambers was vice president/general manager of Space and Intelligence Systems and CEO for Boeing Satellite Systems and recently was assigned to the 787 program. John Peller (prior to retiring from Boeing) served as vice president of Strategic Missile Defense, and was VP and GM for Ground-based Midcourse Missile Defense (previously called National Missile Defense); at Rockwell, Peller was VP of Engineering for the Space Division. Many other former Rockwell executives are in very senior positions, and many of Rockwell's management processes have been adopted within Boeing.

Boeing estimates that about $9 billion of its Integrated Defense Systems sales are directly attributed to the Rockwell businesses or where Rockwell technology and people play a major role. It is clear that the Rockwell businesses and people have fared well as a result of being a part of this aerospace powerhouse.

AUTOMOTIVE

Meritor, Inc. was created by the spin-off in 1997 of Rockwell Automotive. The company consisted of two major segments – Commercial Vehicle Systems and Light Vehicle Systems. Sales that year were about $3.3 billion. The company operated 46 manufacturing plants worldwide, as well as 19 technical and sales offices in 15 countries. The company acquired the heavy-duty axle manufacturing operations in Sweden of Volvo, a leading replacement parts manufacturer for heavy-duty trucks, trailer and tractors, and also acquired the heavy vehicle braking systems business of LucasVarity, a British company. In 2000, Meritor merged with Arvin Industries to form ArvinMeritor, Inc. The new company had combined sales of about $7 billion in 2001.

Over the years, the company has significantly reduced its Light Vehicle segment through a series of divestitures in order to focus on body systems (roof and door systems), chassis systems (suspension systems and modules and ride control products), and wheel products for passenger cars, all-terrain vehicles, light and medium trucks and sport utility vehicles supplied to the OEMs. Commercial Vehicle is the largest and most profitable business.

41. Meritor heritage

Larry Yost was the first chairman and CEO and retired in 2004. Charles "Chip" McClure joined the company and replaced Yost at that time. During its roughly 10 years as a public company, ArvinMeritor has significantly enhanced its product offerings through acquisitions and internal development. Many aggressive business development initiatives have been focused on growth outside the U.S., particularly in Asia (including numerous "green field" new plants and joint ventures). Numerous businesses have been divested in order to put more focus and resources on the best opportunities for profitable growth.

Considerable effort also has been directed to substantially improve the cost structure and global manufacturing footprint through plant closings, new plants, and many internal programs focused on operational efficiencies and quality. Many product lines have been divested. The entire automotive industry worldwide is, of course, going through major changes and difficulties, and the company has moved aggressively to adapt and find opportunities.

With all of the restructuring/divestiture initiatives, the financials are best understood on a continuing operations basis. After all the changes, the business in 2007 had sales of about $6.5 billion and was about at break-even in profitability, before charges for discontinued businesses. EBITDA was about $250 million, essentially all from the Commercial Vehicle business. For the most recent quarter (ending in March 2008), volume was running at an annual rate of about $7.1 billion (Commercial Vehicle Systems at about $4.8 billion and Light Vehicle Systems at $2.3 billion) with net income at an annual rate of about $80 million ... the company was projecting steady future improvement with all of the restructuring and operational improvements benefiting. Commercial Vehicle Systems was producing EBITDA at an annual rate of about $350 million and Light Vehicle Systems at a rate of about $80 million. Table 1 below illustrates these results:

Table 1 ArvinMeritor Current Operating Results

(Annualized First-Half 2008 Rates)

	CVS	LVS	Total
Sales ($B)	$4.8	$2.3	$7.1
EBITDA ($M)	$336.0	$76.0	$412.0
Net Income ($M)			$80.0

The latest major event was the announcement in May 2008 that the Light Vehicle Systems business will be spun-off to the ArvinMeritor shareowners by early 2009. Thus, the Automotive businesses would proceed as two very focused global entities serving Commercial Vehicle markets (ArvinMeritor – ARM) and Light Vehicle markets (ArvinInnovation – ARVI).

Separating these businesses and implementing ArvinMeritor's Performance Plus initiatives are major steps in its transformation to build a stronger, more competitive company for the future.

The LVS spin-off transaction is about refocusing the company on its core operations. ArvinMeritor is creating two independent companies that will allow each to grow and prosper in a way that is consistent with the business mix and industry opportunities of each company.

ArvinInnovation and ArvinMeritor will benefit from stronger competitive positions, improved financial flexibility and enhanced strategic focus on their respective core businesses and growth opportunities.

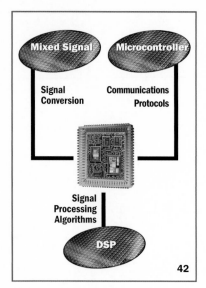

42. A graphical representation of the primary functions of Conexant systems on a chip

The LVS group has the right leadership team, solid financial structure, market leading products, diversified customer mix and global reach to grow this new company as a market leader going forward.

LVS will continue to be a leading global supplier of dynamic motion and control automotive systems, providing cost-effective, highly engineered automotive systems that enhance vehicle functionality and performance.

CVS will continue to be a market leader in drivetrain and braking components and systems for heavy- and medium-duty trucks, trailers, buses, off-highway commercial vehicles and government heavy-duty vehicles, and the commercial vehicle aftermarket.

The Rockwell shareowner value is 25 percent of ARM (ArvinMeritor) stock price per share of Rockwell. ARM, adjusted for various transactions, sells for about $15 in August 2008 and has ranged from about $10 per share to $30 per share for the last 10 years. After the Light Vehicle transaction, the Rockwell shareowner value will be 25 percent of ARM plus 25 percent of the value of ARVI (the new Light Vehicle Systems company).

ELECTRONICS

After the Aerospace and Automotive transactions, the continuing Rockwell became a diversified group of Electronics businesses. As discussed earlier, the electronics businesses had been important drivers of growth and profitability within Rockwell for many years. The avionics and communications business had been built around the acquisition of Collins in the 1970s, and the Automation business had been built around the acquisition of Allen-Bradley in 1985. The semiconductor business, however, was developed within Rockwell, combining the technology and products from the Rockwell Science Center, the electronic segment of North American Aviation (Autonetics), and various system and device capabilities of Collins.

The semiconductor business became one of the major entrepreneurial initiatives within Rockwell and continued as such as Conexant, Mindspeed and Skyworks. Because of the major high risk/high potential and very entrepreneurial/innovative initiative that was undertaken in these very fast-moving advanced technology growth markets, the Semiconductor story will be told here in a different nature and with a bit more detail.

THE SEMICONDUCTOR BUSINESSES

The Rockwell semiconductor business that in 1999 became the public company Conexant was described earlier and could best be characterized as a communications systems business where the products are implemented in very large scale (VLSI) integrated circuits (ICs).

Within Rockwell, the business grew during the 1990s from about $200 million to $1.6 billion in 1997. The majority of this growth was driven by the company's leading market share in modems for Personal Computers (PCs) and facsimile machines, implemented as semiconductor chipsets and sold by the tens of millions to OEMs worldwide. With this rapid growth came a significant business dependence on the overall modem market segment. To reduce this dependence and to address new growth markets, semiconductor product line acquisitions were made in wide-area networking, satellite and cable communications, wireless handsets and PC video applications. In 1998 and before these acquisitions were contributing meaningfully, a major market share battle with a competitor resulted in rapid modem price erosion, driving a significant revenue decline to $1.2 billion and a swing to operating losses. Despite these difficulties, Conexant was spun-out to shareholders as an independent company in January 1999. The rationale for this spin was described earlier. The spin-out was well received by investors and, at the time, was the largest transaction in the history of the semiconductor industry, with a valuation of $1.8 billion.

Over its history the semiconductor market has been characterized by dramatic business cycles, and the Conexant spin was into an (unexpected) up-cycle. In its first year as a standalone company, the modem business stabilized, and the expansion business areas previously mentioned delivered very strong growth. Calendar 1999 saw a revenue growth of 25 percent over the prior year, with the expansion businesses growing 50 percent and contributing more than half of the company's revenue.

This period was part of what is now referred to as the Telecom/Internet Bubble, and Conexant was a direct beneficiary. As the company's rapid growth continued into early 2000, Conexant's stock price reached almost $135, roughly 15 times the company's spin-out level, delivering a market value of $30 billion, which was three times the market cap of the Rockwell parent at the time. For those investors who understood the dramatic cycles of the semiconductor industry, or recognized the Telecom Bubble for what it would become, or were just lucky, an exit from Conexant around this time captured an exceptional return.

During 2000, Conexant continued to execute its bold but risky strategy of rapid portfolio and technology expansion. The company consummated more than 10 acquisitions in furtherance of its "Five Platforms" strategy that was designed to create the industry-wide leader in communication and media processing applications.

A more detailed characterization of Conexant's products and focused business strategy can be found in Appendices 2 and 3.

Conexant's largest bet to this point in terms of product development resources and acquisition investments was in the Internet Infrastructure market. The Internet Infrastructure business unit of Conexant grew its revenues by 100 percent in 2000 over 1999, to approximately $600 million, and was projecting revenues of $1 billion for 2001.

Instead, the sobering reality of 2001 was the collapse of Telecom and Internet mania and was the most abrupt and deepest downturn in the entire history of the semiconductor industry. The companies most hurt were those with large Telecom and Internet exposure, and Conexant was hit hard. Revenues in 2001 declined by almost half to $1.1 billion, and losses amounted to $1.5 billion, including large restructuring charges from business resizing actions and non-cash goodwill devaluations from the recent acquisitions.

The dramatically different market dynamics of Conexant's various businesses during the 2000-2001 period drove a major re-evaluation of the company's over-arching strategy. The analysis attempted to determine the path forward for Conexant that would deliver the greatest shareowner value. The previous vision of a large semiconductor player addressing the full set of key communications and media processing markets was replaced by a vision of a family of smaller, market-focused, independent companies. Market focused companies were selected because the data at the time clearly demonstrated a valuation "discount" for portfolio breadth and a valuation "premium" for focus.

Focused Business Creation Strategy

In Conexant's case, the natural market-focused segments were Internet Infrastructure, Cellular Phones and Home Communications and Media Processing. After a great deal of discussion, it was decided that Conexant should, therefore, divide into a family of separate and independent companies, and this became known to the Conexant Board of Directors and employees as the Focused Business Creation (FBC) strategy.

A key principle of the new FBC strategy was that the best long-term company performance was achieved when semiconductor product "design" was separated from semiconductor "manufacturing," at least for products that utilized mainstream semiconductor processes

43. 8-inch Silicon Wafer for Specialty Foundry Processes

(called CMOS technologies). Companies that did not do their own wafer manufacturing were called "fabless" (since they did not own wafer fabrication (fab) facilities), and this new class of semiconductor companies was becoming quite successful. At this time in the industry, when a new semiconductor company was started, fabless was the clear choice. But for existing companies with wafer fabs, it was very difficult to devise a successful "transition" to fabless. This is because a wafer fab is only profitable when it is loaded close to capacity, and when a company begins to shift to outside manufacturing, their internal fab operating costs skyrocket (driven by the high fixed costs).

Conexant solved this problem in a very innovative way. In early 2002, it created a new company called Jazz Semiconductor, that provided wafer manufacturing services to Conexant, as well as the future spin-off companies Skyworks and Mindspeed, but also offered its manufacturing services to other semiconductor companies. Jazz was formed in partnership with the Carlyle Group, a prestigious private equity firm that made a $50 million investment. In 2006, Jazz was purchased by a public company called Acquicor, and Conexant received another $100 million for its remaining ownership share. Conexant was an innovator and a market leader in this manufacturing transition, being the first significant "fabbed" semiconductor company to successfully make the move to "fabless."

In the summer of 2002, Conexant continued its FBC strategy and created the cellular handset focused company called Skyworks Solutions through a spin-merge transaction with Alpha Industries. In 2003, it formed the Internet Infrastructure focused company called Mindspeed Technologies through a spin-out. In this process, the continuing Conexant became a company focused on home PC and set-top box applications. Table 2 shows the revenues of each of these companies from their formation to the present.

Table 2 **Semiconductor Businesses Sales** ($ Millions)

Fiscal Year	Conexant	Skyworks	Mindspeed
1998	$1,200		
1999	1,444		
2000	2,103		
2001	1,062		
2002	602	$457	
2003	600	617	$82
2004	902	784	119
2005	722	792	112
2006	970	774	136
2007	808	741	128

Skyworks

In the process of developing Conexant's Focused Business Creation strategy, it became clear that the products and technologies that Conexant had developed in wireless applications would support the establishment of an independent company. A major asset of this new business would be a fast-growing set of products that performed the power amplification function in digital cellular phones. This capability was derived from a specialty semiconductor process technology called Gallium Arsenide (GaAs) that was originally developed in Rockwell through contract work for the Defense Advanced Research Projects Agency (DARPA). The initial DARPA interest was to develop very high-speed semiconductor circuits for military applications. In the early '90s, entrepreneurial engineering and marketing talent identified the potential application of this GaAs technology to commercial power amplification challenges. These entrepreneurs attracted the interest of another nearby innovative company, Qualcomm, for whom they developed a power amplifier product that for several years was used in all of for their new CDMA digital cellular phones. Conexant expanded upon this wireless application by developing chips that performed the radio frequency transmit-and-receive function, as well as central processor chips for cell phones. The cellular market was expected to have long-term, high-growth potential, and the best path for the establishment of a new independent wireless company was studied. It turned out that an existing company, called Alpha Industries, held complementary technology and market positions and was interested in a combination. The result was a transaction in which Conexant spun its wireless assets out as a separate company owned by the Conexant shareholders, and then this company simultaneously merged with Alpha Industries to create what is called Skyworks Solutions. In this process, the Conexant shareowners (and therefore the Rockwell shareowners who owned the spun-out Conexant shares) held approximately 65 percent of the new Skyworks company.

Since its spinout, Skyworks has become a world leader in addressing the cellular handset market. Today, 80 percent of the cellular phones in the world are provided by the top five manufacturers, Nokia, Samsung, Motorola, Sony Ericsson and LG, and Skyworks is a major provider to them all. For cellular "front-end" products (power amplifiers and band switches), Skyworks has only one significant competitor, RF Micro Devices, and the company has consistently outperformed this competitor in terms of product gross margins (product market value compared to cost), as well as operating profitability and cash flow. As Skyworks continues to grow its front-end market share, it has been investing in diversifying its product portfolio into related wireless as well as analog/mixed signal markets. In terms of market value, Skyworks moves with investor sentiment on the cellular market, and its market capitalization has been volatile, with swings between approximately $500 million and $2 billion. In early FY2008, sales are at an annual rate of about $850 million with positive cash flow, and the Skyworks outlook is positive. (www.skyworks.com)

Mindspeed

Once Conexant's Focused Business Creation strategy was defined in mid-2000, the formation of what would become Mindspeed was clearly identified as the first implementation step. This was because companies that were focused on telecom applications were receiving extraordinary shareholder value premiums at that time. In the fall of 2000, the consensus of the most reputable Wall Street investment banks was that Mindspeed would have approximately a $10 billion market capitalization upon its spin-off. As mentioned previously, however, the Telecom Bubble that was producing such enormous valuations burst within weeks of the scheduled launch of Mindspeed's Initial Public Offering (IPO). Had the timing been 30 days sooner, Mindspeed would have had many unhappy new shareholders who had purchased at the IPO price, but the company would have had about $1 billion of offering proceeds to weather the "Telecom Nuclear Winter" that was about to unfold. Instead, Conexant had to decide what to do with a business that had peaked at quarterly revenues of almost $250 million but was on its way to a (much deeper than expected) bottom of $15 million a quarter. Management and the Conexant Board decided that Mindspeed had a number of enduring assets that should result in solid (but not bubble) shareholder value over time. These business assets included products that delivered (and their derivatives still deliver) very high gross margins of 65 percent (compared to Conexant or Skyworks margins of 40-45 percent), and customer design wins that generate 5-10 years of steady revenue (compared to standard semiconductor

44. Mindspeed headquarters, Newport Beach, CA

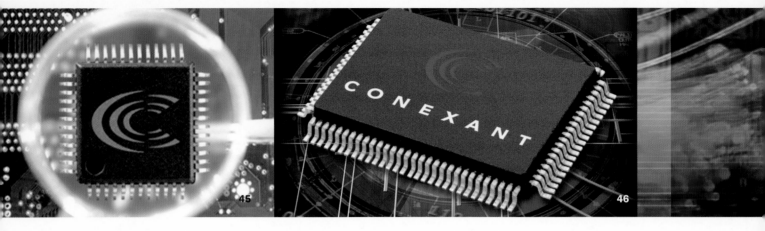

45. - 46. Conexant-developed semiconductor solutions

product lifecycles of 12-18 months). As a result, Conexant maintained Mindspeed as a wholly owned subsidiary, reduced operating costs substantially, but maintained core product development investments. By early 2003, the worst of the telecom collapse was over, and Mindspeed revenues had first stabilized and then began to grow again. Conexant completed a 100 percent spin-out to its shareholders in the summer of 2003, and Mindspeed finally became an independent company. Once again, the volatility of the semiconductor industry demonstrated itself with Mindspeed's initial market valuation of approximately $200 million growing over the next 12 months to more than $1 billion. And, once again, the Mindspeed-Conexant-Rockwell shareowner that appreciated the cyclical nature of the semiconductor industry and acted accordingly, was handsomely rewarded.

Mindspeed has steadily broadened its market penetration in its original core markets of voice transport, carrier Voice Over Internet Protocol (VOIP) and optical transmission, but the telecom semiconductor space has not returned to high growth. Mindspeed has remained entrepreneurial, however, and has invested outside the telecom infrastructure space by leveraging its core technologies in innovative ways. For example, it now has business units that apply optical transmission technology for chip-to-chip communication and leverage telecom crosspoint switch technology in the high-definition video creation and storage fields. Although it has taken longer than even the most pessimistic initial post-bubble forecasts, the company is now profitable and cash flow positive. The annual revenue run-rate for Mindspeed is now approximately $150 million, and multi-year growth rates of 15-20 percent per year are expected. Considering Mindspeed's high product gross margins, if these revenue growth plans are achieved, a highly profitable and highly valued company will result. (www.mindspeed.com)

The Continuing Conexant

After the spin-offs of both Skyworks and Mindspeed, the Conexant business was comprised of two market segments. The first segment was based on the heritage analog modem business for both facsimile and PC applications and which remained a market share leader and extremely profitable. Since its spin-out, Conexant had expanded this communications position to higher speeds by developing DSL chipsets. In the process, the company built a number two market share position in broadband modem products for PCs and Internet access. The second segment was focused on chipsets for digital satellite and cable set-top box products, a market space that was growing with the increased adoption of digital TV. The core technology and talent for this initiative came as a result of the acquisition of Brooktree in 1996 by the Rockwell Semiconductor business.

By the fall of 2004, a year after completion of the Mindspeed spin, the continuing Conexant had been growing steadily, with improving margins, and had an annualized revenue run-rate of approximately $750 million and was delivering 10 percent operating profit. At this point, Conexant merged with GlobespanVirata, which proved to be extremely challenging. GlobespanVirata held the leading position in DSL chipsets for both consumer and carrier

applications, and it had recently acquired a wireless LAN (Wi-Fi) business. The strategic rationale for the merger was to create a clear leader in both narrowband (analog) and broadband (DSL) chipsets and to be one of only two semiconductor companies (the other being Broadcom) with the technology and market positions to capitalize on the coming merger of broadband communications and broadband video (DSL routers combined with set-top boxes to deliver integrated Internet access and digital television). The transaction was considered a merger-of-equals, which meant roughly balanced headcount and leadership from each company. The merger partners had been headquartered on opposite coasts and had very different company cultures. For these and other reasons, the required process of business prioritization and the alignment of product roadmaps were executed badly, and business performance suffered significantly as 2005 progressed. In retrospect, the strategic rationale for the Conexant/GlobespanVirata merger was sound. But the gap between the merger concept and the merger reality, most particularly in the area of the merger integration, was enormous. Despite the launch of several recovery initiatives since early 2006, the Conexant business remains challenged.

Conexant currently is undergoing a further major restructuring – its Broadband Media Processing business (digital satellite, cable, and terrestrial set-top box solutions) was sold to NXP Semiconductors, a Phillips spin-off. This leaves Conexant as a supplier of analog modem-based products (the heritage business) and DSL broadband modem products. Sales from these businesses are about $450 million and will be profitable with positive cash flow. Conexant will be challenged to develop and/or acquire products that can provide more growth opportunities than these businesses.

The semiconductor business grown within Rockwell has been a major entrepreneurial initiative. Skyworks and Mindspeed are well positioned for long-term growth and enhanced shareowner returns. Conexant, as now restructured will be profitable but must prove it can achieve a growth trajectory. (www.conexant.com)

47. Mindspeed expanded into broadcast video and optical transmission markets

48. Mindspeed's Comcerto® brand of Voice Over Internet Protocol (VOIP) processors

ROCKWELL COLLINS

Rockwell Collins' 75-year heritage is filled with stories of determination, resolve, and resiliency – as well as products recognized across the globe for distinctive quality and state-of-the-art technology.

Rockwell Collins' predecessor, Collins Radio Company, was founded by Arthur Collins in 1933 in Cedar Rapids, Iowa, and initially designed and produced short wave radio equipment. The company enjoyed rapid growth during World War II and continued to expand its work in all phases of the communications field, while broadening its technology focus into numerous other disciplines, including communications for America's space program.

Rockwell International acquired Collins Radio Company. Under Rockwell International, the Collins businesses were split into separate divisions for defense and commercial products – with separate organizations and support functions – essentially aligned with the other businesses of Rockwell. These businesses operated successfully for over 20 years. But after the sale of the company's aerospace business to Boeing in 1996, the Collins divisions were once again joined, allowing them to leverage commercial technologies for government applications – and vice versa.

Over the next five years, the Collins businesses did a remarkable job optimizing the components around a shared infrastructure and technology base that accelerated its growth and profitability. Ultimately, this reunion also helped prepare the company for one of its most challenging transitions to date: standing alone.

Present-day Rockwell Collins, Inc. spun off from Rockwell International in June 2001, and became a public and independent company, trading on the New York Stock Exchange under the new ticker symbol: "COL." Clay Jones was named president and CEO. Don Beall was asked by Clay and the Rockwell board to be non-CEO chairman of the Board to help the new company get launched. Clay assumed the additional role of chairman a year later with Beall becoming chairman of the board's executive committee.

Then came a perfect storm: a rare confluence of management and market challenges – each a formidable test in its own right. First, the company's management team was leading a newly independent, publicly held company for the first time, with new stakeholders and greater accountability. Then – just 10 weeks after the spin-off – the company was plunged into a fundamentally changed post 9/11 world that included a precipitous drop in the commercial aviation market.

It was a trial by fire. But Rockwell Collins' management team, led by Clay Jones, president and chief executive officer, showed a strong capacity for decisive and strategic action.

This time of sharply declining OEM orders in the commercial market would test the company. But an extraordinary leadership team, combined with nearly 70 years of brand equity, and several pivotal business strategies, would help the fledgling standalone organization prevail.

Despite the great uncertainty of the times, Rockwell Collins' leadership team made early decisions – before many in the industry – based on what they thought the market would yield. Then they acted quickly to size Rockwell Collins and shift resources to better align with a new environment, including salary freezes and workforce reductions.

But the perfect storm continued. The terrorist attacks were followed by a weak economy, wars in Afghanistan and Iraq, and a SARS epidemic, all of which further impacted Rockwell Collins' commercial customers.

How did Rockwell Collins weather this – and subsequent – storms? By leveraging the strengths acquired and embedded in its culture while part of Rockwell International: a balanced business and highly integrated organizational structure, a commitment to innovation, and a relentless focus on customers through operational excellence.

Each of these strengths enabled the company to capitalize on opportunities to grow the business.

Adding Value

Rockwell Collins has been a major contributor to the value achieved by the Rockwell share-owner. The following charts summarize the financials of the company for FY 2001-2007, the period following the spin-off.

Collins' market value increased from $2.6 to $12.2 billion from the spin in 2001 until the end of FY '07. The stock price increased from just under $15 in September 2001 to just over $76 in September 2007 (all of the Rockwell-related businesses have fiscal years ending in September). With the weak economy and market correction, the August 31, 2008, comparable values are $8.3 billion market value and a stock price of $57, including accumulated dividends.

Chart 11 shows that Collins generated more than $3 billion from operations during its first seven years as a public company. For the same period, about $500 million was paid in dividends, CAPEX was about $800 million, and a similar amount was invested in acquisitions.

The impressive cash flow provided the resources for share repurchases of about $1.8 billion, a major reduction in outstanding shares (from 183.8 million at the spin-off to 165.8 million as of September 30, 2007), further benefiting shareowners.

Not shown on the chart, but equally impressive, the company invested more than $4 billion in R&D during this period, or about 18 percent of sales between company and customer-funded programs (40% and 60%, respectively).

Chart 12 shows a summary of the sales, net income, and EPS for the period. The numbers truly do speak for themselves—fiscal year 2008 sales are forecast at about $4.8 billion with EPS of $4.04 (consensus analyst estimate as of July 2008); clearly a departure from the current, we think depressed, stock market valuation.

Chart 10 Rockwell Collins Market Value & Stock Price

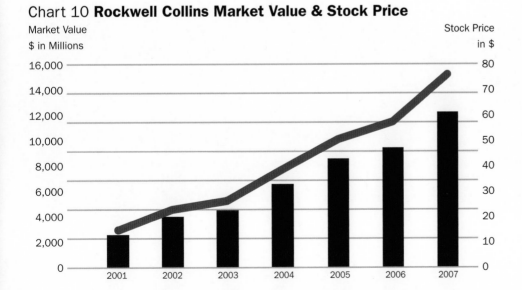

Market Value
$ in Millions

Stock Price
in $

■ Market Value ■ Stock Price incl. accumulated dividends

Chart 11 **Rockwell Collins Cash Flows 2001 - 2007**
$ in Millions

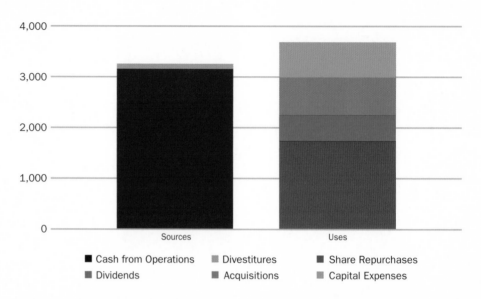

Cash from Operations ◾ Divestitures ◾ Share Repurchases
◾ Dividends ◾ Acquisitions ◾ Capital Expenses

Chart 12 **Rockwell Collins Sales, Net Income and EPS 2001- 2007**
$ in Millions except EPS

Earnings per Share in $

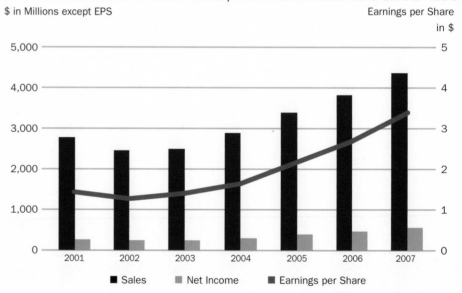

◾ Sales ◾ Net Income ◾ Earnings per Share

How does Rockwell Collins continue to achieve record growth despite market downturns? Primarily, it comes down to customer balance; an efficient organizational structure; a culture of innovation; unrelenting customer focus; continuing dedication to operational excellence and Lean principles; and smart growth.

Balanced and Integrated Organizational Structure

Rockwell Collins serves a highly diverse and balanced mix of customers through two (now reunited) business units: Government Systems and Commercial Systems.

In both businesses, Rockwell Collins is a key supplier to domestic and international original equipment manufacturers and aftermarket customers. Commercial customers include operators of airlines, regional carriers and business aircraft, and the manufacturers that serve

49. Multiscan Weather Radar

50. In-Flight Entertainment System

them worldwide. Government customers include all branches of the U.S. military—as well as many foreign militaries. This diversified business mix provides stability and flexibility in a dynamic environment, with a well-balanced customer base spanning these markets. It also gives the company the ability to offset cyclical declines in one business with growth in another.

Jones and his leadership team leveraged this diversified business mix into a highly integrated business model. Throughout the entire enterprise, Rockwell Collins was structured with common processes, facilities, and resources to enable the cross-leveraging of technologies, products and capabilities for efficient use of assets. This integration at the product and system level meant lower development costs—and faster time to market.

And, by leveraging a Shared Services model, the company was able to get more efficiency out of functions like Human Resources, Finance, Operations and others that supported the businesses, and to provide the kind of operating efficiencies needed to better serve customers.

Commitment to Innovation

Rockwell Collins' leadership team also recognized that in order to succeed in a challenging and dynamic marketplace, the company would need to continuously search for ways to upgrade products to serve customers better, build competitive advantage, and encourage growth in the future. As a result, significant investment in research and development became fundamental at the company. This funding has provided both innovative solutions to customers and the ability to deliver leading-edge capabilities in the future.

A highly integrated business model is an advantage here as well. Rockwell Collins' technology centers of excellence and its centralized advanced technology group have allowed the company to effectively leverage technology investments across commercial and government product portfolios. The result? Maximized returns on investment.

That concept led to the successful creation of open systems architecture solutions that could be used to serve customers across market lines. One example was Rockwell Collins' KC-135 Global Air Traffic Management award. This program took advantage of technology first developed for commercial markets, tailored only as necessary to meet specific military needs. This use of existing technology allowed the U.S. Air Force to leverage hundreds of millions of dollars already invested in developing these products for the commercial market.

Key programs in the commercial sector between 2001 and 2008 have been numerous. The company launched the next generation of in-flight entertainment system development, Information Management Systems and Cabin Electronics Systems that led the way in the journey to bring home entertainment and an "office in the sky" to business aircraft. Today, the company's eXchange™ system now brings high speed, broadband connectivity to business jets around the world.

51. Head-up Guidance System®

52. Boeing 787 Dreamliner Flight Deck

53. Airshow 4000 moving map system

In 2007, Rockwell Collins introduced the Venue™ system, its next generation, high definition cabin management system for business jets. The Venue system features digital, high-definition video, a media center, high-definition displays, a programmable switch panel and iPod integration.

Other products on the cutting edge of information delivery include the Integrated Flight Information System, enabling such advanced capabilities as electronic charting, graphical weather and enhanced map overlays on the flight decks of business jets; Rockwell Collins' Core Network Cabinet bringing e-enabled functionality to air transport aircraft; and the Airshow® moving map and Tailwind® television systems for business jets and airlines.

Then there are devices that help pilots see what they could not normally see; products that help take much of the guesswork and risk out of flying. The company's HGS® Head-up Guidance System, Multiscan™ Hazard Detection Systems and Synthetic Vision System are allowing pilots to fly more safely than ever before.

A particularly proud moment for Rockwell Collins' commercial business came when the company was selected to provide avionics and pilot controls for the Boeing 787 Dreamliner. The program represents the most content Rockwell Collins has ever had on a commercial aircraft, and is anticipated to generate revenues in excess of $3 billion over its life.

In 2008, the company captured significant positions on Airbus' new A350XWB, which could generate revenues in excess of $2.5 billion over the life of the program. These positions represent twice as much content than Rockwell Collins has ever had on any Airbus airplane.

At the same time, Rockwell Collins has been extremely successful in expanding its market share in the business and regional segment. Since the spin off in 2001, there have been 17 head-to-head competitions for new business jet avionics positions – and Rockwell Collins has won 16 of them.

The introduction of Pro Line Fusion™ avionics in 2007 has been well-received by customers throughout the world. Bombardier, Cessna, Embraer and Mitsubishi have all chosen Pro Line Fusion avionics for new platforms. Pro Line Fusion avionics offer a flexible architecture providing high reliability with extensive growth capabilities to meet the anticipated future airspace requirements, and to support new technology and feature insertions.

The government business avails itself of many of the same technologies found in the commercial segment. An example is the Common Avionics Architecture System (CAAS) for rotary wing aircraft.

Initially developed for the Special Operations Forces MH-47G Chinook and MH-60L/M Black Hawk aircraft, CAAS is a fully integrated flight and mission management capability that provides exceptional mission effectiveness. As the common digital architecture for rotary

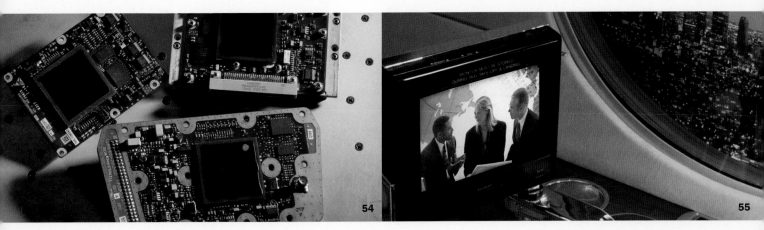

54

55

wing aircraft for the U.S. Army, CAAS is one of the first fully open, non-proprietary systems that completely embraces existing commercial standards on large platforms.

Rockwell Collins has also responded to the military's special needs and requirements. The company has produced and delivered more than 200,000 Defense Advanced Global Positioning System Receivers (DAGR), the gold-standard for U.S. military ground forces as well as GPS receivers for a multitude of other applications including missiles and munitions. The company also produces the government-mandated Selective Availability Anti-Spoofing (SAASM) module, which is required for all future equipment in an effort to better secure military GPS receivers.

Rockwell Collins' ARC-210 is the military standard for VHF communication today, and the company is at the forefront of development of next generation software defined radios for a variety of applications.

Joint ventures, alliances, and teaming relationships with firms including Sandia Labs, Thales, BAE Systems, Elbit and Honeywell have also produced new breakthrough products for government customers.

With rapidly shifting commercial and government markets – and exponential change driven by today's global economy – innovation at Rockwell Collins has become a competitive strength through a combination of a balanced and integrated organization, focused planning, aggressive and consistent funding, organizational leverage, and a culture that makes full use of talented and motivated people.

Relentless Focus on the Customer:
Operational Excellence and Lean Electronics

Rockwell Collins has also been able to weather the storms that have come its way through a strong focus on Operational Excellence and "Lean Electronics." The goal of this initiative was – and is – to better serve customers by carving waste out of the company using the tools of Lean throughout the organization, factory and office alike. Jones and his leadership team knew that their efforts in this area were fundamental to the value today's customers demand, and would be critical for driving ongoing improvements in quality, service, and financial performance.

Once again, the company leveraged this strength, acquired while part of Rockwell International. The company's implementation of Lean tools and techniques in the late 1990s – such as 5S activities, a version of Kaizen events called Radical Process Improvement (RPI), and Lean training and certification programs for employees – provided a solid foundation.

However, as the company's Lean Journey progressed, it became clear that completing independent Lean events in several areas wasn't necessarily changing the dynamics of the

54. Selective Availability Anti-Spoofing (SAASM) module is required for future government equipment to better secure military GPS receivers

55. Airshow 21 cabin electronics system for business aircraft

56. KC-135R aircraft

business. As a result, a new initiative called Core Process Optimization (CPO) was launched to both identify the company's core business processes and to take actions to maximize their efficiency and effectiveness. CPO was a way to apply Lean to the enterprise as a total integrated value stream, involving employees and suppliers as well as customers.

Jones knew that Lean would be crucial to the company's success going forward, and he began a far-reaching and holistic look at the effectiveness of the company's Lean journey.

From this analysis, the company made some course corrections. These involved accelerating the application of Lean tools and principles; making Lean events more efficient and reducing the time from start to result; and more clearly spelling out for each Lean activity a distinct benefit to the customers, shareowner, or employee. Additionally, the course correction found that Rockwell Collins leaders were too frequently delegating lean instead of actively becoming involved. The company's leaders renewed their dedication to leading by example.

As a result of this feedback and other analyses, leaders were required to learn and teach Value Stream Mapping, and be able to align these events with the company's bottom line. Rockwell Collins also revamped its Lean Roadmap to include value streams needing to be optimized. By defining present and future state goals, and pinpointing the specific events needed to accomplish those goals, the company reached a defining moment. Rockwell Collins moved from being a company that holds Lean up as an independent initiative to making Lean a success enabler ingrained in the company's culture.

As Jones and his leadership team defined "what it would take to win" on an enterprise level, they also realized that they needed to identify metrics – every part of the company would have a different role as components of the value stream. The result was a Rockwell Collins Scorecard to provide this visibility, through components such as Customer Acceptance Rate, On-Time Delivery, Sales Growth, Cash Flow from Operations, Return on Invested Capital, and Earnings Per Share, among others.

The next step on Rockwell Collins' Lean Journey came when this leadership team recognized that while the company was optimizing within each core process, it was not necessarily optimizing the value stream across those processes. They identified hand-offs and communication issues that made the enterprise less effective. To ensure that core processes were integrated and working in a continuous flow across the business, the company implemented Life Cycle Value Stream Management (LCVSM), which created clearly defined lines of management authority for Rockwell Collins' product groups. LCVSM, launched in 2004, required extensive changes – new roles and responsibilities, metrics, rewards and recognition, and the implementation of a Lean Cost System to drive better business decisions through more discrete allocation of costs.

The company's Lean outcomes have been, and continue to be, groundbreaking. In just one example, an Accounting project team at Rockwell Collins was able to use tools for variation reduction to achieve an $8.8 million improvement in cash flow related to domestic customers, and $13 million related to international customers. Whether the issue is inventory turns, customer deliveries, backlog, or office processes, making the use of Lean tools a way of life has been able to effect dramatic change throughout the enterprise.

Rockwell Collins' Lean Journey has enabled the company to not only meet commitments to customers, most notably through dramatic improvements in quality and on-time delivery, but also to win programs and meet its financial commitments.

Growth

From Rockwell Collins' early steps as an independent, public company, Jones established aggressive long-term goals for the enterprise. Those goals included annual sales growth of 10 percent, with 8 percent organic growth; earnings-per-share growth in the range of 13 to 15 percent; cash flow from operations of 100 to 130 percent of net income; and return on invested capital of 20 to 25 percent. Rockwell Collins' performance has been at, or better than, those long-term targets for four consecutive years.

Since the spin-off in 2001, Rockwell Collins also focused on leveraging its core strengths and expanding them through acquisitions and alliances to provide new capabilities to its current and future customers. Recent acquisitions have included: Athena Technologies, Inc., which enables Rockwell Collins to deliver total awareness and automation to both manned and unmanned systems through communications, sensors, navigation and controls; Information Technology and Applications Corporation, which expanded the company's ability to provide users access and use of near real-time geospatial intelligence and other mission-critical information; Anzus, Inc., and IP Unwired, both further augmenting Rockwell Collins' Network-Centric Operations capabilities; Evans & Sutherland's simulation business, strengthening Rockwell Collins' simulation and training capabilities with a full line of professional hardware and software designed to create highly realistic visual images for simulation, training, engineering, and other applications; TELDIX GmbH, broadening Rockwell Collins' European presence; NLX LLC, establishing Rockwell Collins' simulation and training business; Airshow, Inc., expanding Rockwell Collins' cabin electronics offerings; and Communication Solutions, Inc., strengthening Rockwell Collins' product portfolio for customers in the areas of signals intelligence and surveillance solutions.

Jones and his leadership team have also implemented an array of actions – ranging from diversity strategies, to Science, Technology, Engineering, and Mathematics (STEM) education initiatives – to ensure Rockwell Collins will be able to attract, retain and develop the people needed to grow the company in an ever-changing global economy.

Rockwell Collins continues to pursue its shared vision of "Working together creating the most trusted source of communication and aviation electronic solutions" and fulfilling its brand promise: Building trust every day with customers, employees, shareowners, suppliers and others who rely on Rockwell Collins.

These trusted relationships, combined with lean, streamlined processes; a strong commitment to innovation; and the successful operation of a balanced and integrated business model continue to be the driving forces behind the company's ability to deliver consistently improving financial results. (www.rockwellcollins.com)

ROCKWELL AUTOMATION

The surviving Rockwell business after the spin-off of Rockwell Collins became Rockwell Automation. Rockwell Automation had evolved within Rockwell starting with the acquisition of Allen-Bradley in 1985, Reliance Electric in 1994, and numerous strategic transactions to capitalize internally and externally over the years. Rockwell had chosen, as mentioned earlier, to invest heavily in this business with the strategic intent of taking this business to its full potential with a very long-term attitude. As we will see, this business, like Rockwell Collins has performed in a very exemplary manner and has richly rewarded the Rockwell shareowner. This was possible due to very capable and highly motivated people.

The following charts provide an overview of the important financials for Rockwell Automation from 2001-2007. When Collins was spun-off in 2001, the remaining Rockwell became Rockwell Automation.

Chart 13 **Rockwell Automation Market Value & Stock Price**

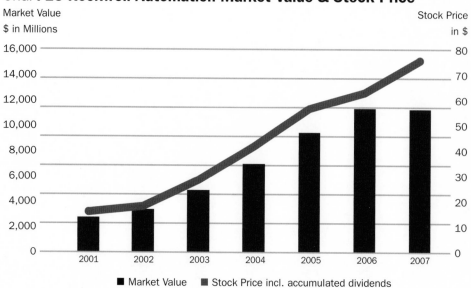

Chart 14 **Rockwell Automation Cash Flows 2001 - 2007**

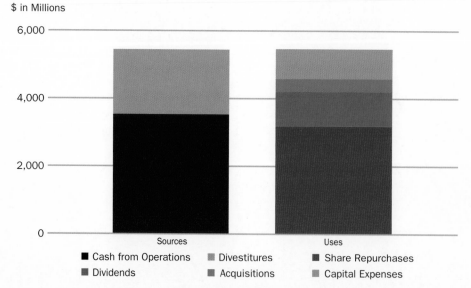

Market value increased from $2.7 billion to $11.2 billion during the period ending September 2007. The stock, including accumulated dividends, increased from about $15 to over $77 during the same period. As with Rockwell Collins, the weak economy and market correction resulted in August 31, 2008, comparable values of $6.8 billion market value and a stock price of $54, including accumulated dividends.

The business produced $3.4 billion in operating cash flow and added to that about $1.8 billion from divestitures, primarily the Power Systems business acquired as part of the Reliance Electric acquisition of 1994.

Uses during the period included CAPEX of about $900 million, dividends of about $1 billion, and acquisitions of about $400 million. The company also had the resources for stock repurchases of about $3.2 billion.

Chart 15 summarizes sales, net income, and EPS for the 2001-2007 period. The numbers speak for themselves! Fiscal year 2008 sales are forecast at about $5.6 billion with EPS of $4 (consensus analyst estimate as of July 2008); clearly another "disconnect" between business performance and the market.

Rockwell Automation has provided an excellent summary of their life as a new public company, as follows:

Technology and Business Transformation:
The Story of Rockwell Automation

The birth of Rockwell Automation in 2001 represented the culmination of Rockwell International's five-year-long strategic divestiture of its business units – aerospace, automotive, electronics, semiconductor and printing – into highly focused companies better able to increase shareowner and customer value.

When Rockwell spun off its Rockwell Collins unit to shareowners as a new public company, the remaining business, which continued to carry the legal and financial heritage of the original Rockwell International, was re-named Rockwell Automation.

Chart 15 Rockwell Automation Sales, Net Income and
EPS 2001 - 2007

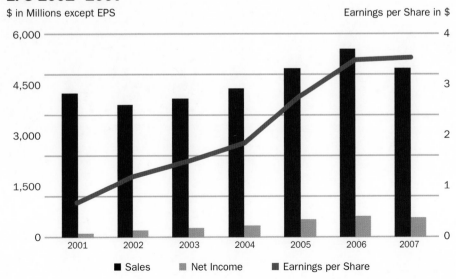

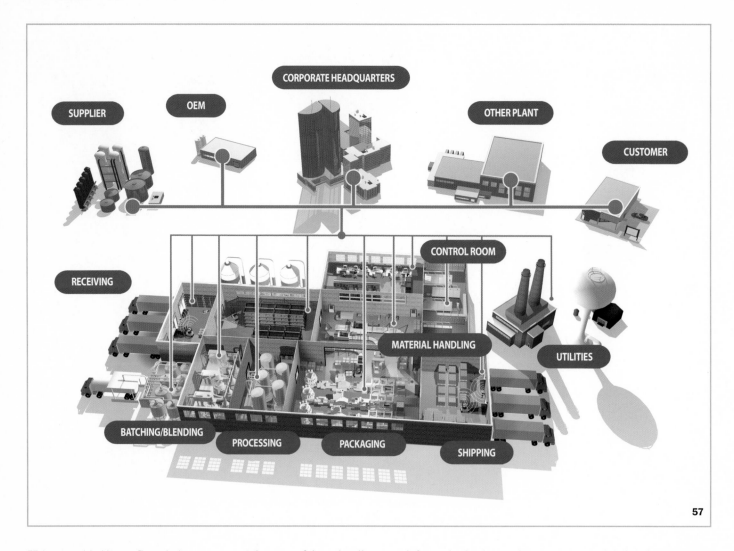

SUPPLIER

OEM

CORPORATE HEADQUARTERS

OTHER PLANT

CUSTOMER

RECEIVING

CONTROL ROOM

MATERIAL HANDLING

UTILITIES

BATCHING/BLENDING

PROCESSING

PACKAGING

SHIPPING

57

57. Integrated Architecture™ – a single solution for information and automation.

The powerful Rockwell name, defining leadership and innovation in global technology, was now aligned in a very visible manner with the world of industrial automation. The company continues to be listed on the New York Stock Exchange (NYSE) under the symbol ROK.

This event marked the launch of Rockwell Automation's own strategic transformation – from a U.S.-based hardware company to a more global technology-driven enterprise focused on integrated architecture, control products, and automation solutions and services.

That evolution, from 2001 to 2007 unfolded under the leadership of two successive chief executives, Don Davis and Keith Nosbusch. Both had built their careers at Allen-Bradley and brought forward the deeply entrenched values and ethical standards that were hallmarks of that century-old business.

Davis began his career with Allen-Bradley in 1963 as an engineering sales trainee. At the time of the 1985 acquisition of Allen-Bradley by Rockwell International, Davis was a senior vice president, working under the leadership of Tracy O'Rourke. In 1989, Davis was named president of Allen-Bradley, and he was appointed president of Rockwell International in 1996. His appointments as CEO and chairman of Rockwell followed in 1997 and 1998, respectively, and he retired in 2005 after serving more than 42 years with the company he helped shape and prepare for a dominant position as a global provider of industrial automation.

Nosbusch, another career employee from the Allen-Bradley legacy, started with the company in 1974 as an applications engineer and moved through the ranks of increasingly responsible roles within Allen-Bradley following the 1985 acquisition by Rockwell. Davis named him

president of Rockwell's Control Systems business in 1998. He was appointed to succeed Davis as chairman of Rockwell Automation in 2004, a position he continues to hold today.

These two leaders shared a common vision for growth and value creation: build a business model focused on ever-higher levels of differentiation through technology leadership and innovation. They took a plant-wide view of Rockwell Automation's ability to add customer value and made the centerpiece of Rockwell's offerings the integrated control and information architecture capable of connecting the customers' entire manufacturing enterprise.

They realized this vision by investing dramatically in a unique open technology known as Logix; significantly expanding the company's footprint beyond discrete control and evolving into plant-wide control, safety and information. In so doing, Davis and Nosbusch thoughtfully re-shaped the company so that by 2007, it was a pure-play industrial automation business with leading product, services and manufacturing solutions expertise.

Expanding Served Markets Through Technology Leadership

First introduced in 1999, the Logix architecture has had a revolutionary impact on manufacturing. Logix is an integrated control and information technology that gives manufacturers the ability to integrate multiple control disciplines, such as discrete, motion, batch and continuous process, motor, and safety, on a single platform – providing the foundation for a single plant-wide automation system. The Logix architecture also allows access to critical information linking the plant floor to the enterprise business systems and its global supply chain by combining these control disciplines with a contemporary software platform using open, unmodified standard connectivity over Ethernet.

Logix was the single largest R&D investment in Rockwell Automation's history, and it has been critical to the company's growth and revenue diversification, not only because of its financial success, but also because of its plant-wide control and information capability.

Execution of Rockwell Automation's plant-wide control strategy has been the key to addressing the automation needs of customers' in consumer and resource-based industries. Rockwell had traditionally served discrete manufacturers, such as the automotive industry. Logix allowed Rockwell Automation to address the process control requirements of the food, beverage, pharmaceutical, oil and gas industries, and others, extending its market reach vertically to a new set of customers. By 2007, process had become Rockwell Automation's largest growth initiative.

The Logix architecture has also led to growth in the evolving manufacturing information software market. Its FactoryTalk integrated production and management performance software suite allows customers to seamlessly integrate plant-floor data with their business systems and supply chains to increase speed, productivity, improve asset utilization, and make more effective real-time business decisions.

58. With the FactoryTalk® integrated suite of highly scalable, modular software applications, you can integrate your factory floor

59. The Logix Control Platform provides fully integrated, scalable solutions for the full range of automation disciplines, including discrete, motion, process and batch control, drive control, and safety applications

Original Equipment Manufacturers (OEM) machine builders have provided the third leg of the Logix growth initiative. OEMs are under extreme cost pressure and need to reduce time to market as they introduce new machines. As an outgrowth of its industry vertical strategy, Rockwell Automation began to capitalize on the scalability of Logix and bundle that technology with motion, safety, and services to meet the unique needs of machine builders and help customers enhance their machine performance and improve their bottom lines.

In sum, the convergence of discrete, process and information in a safe and secure environment has become a game-changing opportunity for Rockwell Automation to expand its plant-wide footprint and capitalize on new technologies and applications.

A number of important partnerships emerged during this period to deliver a broader portfolio of products and set of solutions to meet customer demand. A few representative highlights include:

- In 2003, Rockwell Automation began to partner with IBM to provide the global automotive manufacturing and life sciences industries with collaborative technologies to enhance information flow.

- In 2005, the company began to work together with Endress+Hauser, the world's largest independent supplier of process instrumentation, to provide customers with more convenient, standards-compliant methods for configuring a wide range of process instruments. Customers' expect process suppliers to deliver solutions that include instrumentation as part of the total package.

- And in 2007, Rockwell partnered with Internet networking solutions provider Cisco to optimize network integration of Information Technology and manufacturing across the factory floor and throughout the enterprise. This relationship addresses the ongoing network convergence with commercial grade off-the-shelf Ethernet technology onto the plant floor; bringing together the enterprise-level security expertise of Cisco with Rockwell Automation's expertise in real-time control applications.

Driving growth in the process, manufacturing information and global OEM markets will continue to be the cornerstones of Rockwell Automation's focus on served market expansion and revenue diversification.

Enhancing Market Access Through Global Expansion

As the manufacturing world shifted its center of gravity toward emerging markets, Rockwell Automation shifted as well. The company's investment in global market expansion has been a hallmark of its growth since 2001, designed to further diversify revenue, support productivity and supply chain simplification objectives, and improve the company's ability to meet customers' expectations.

Rockwell Automation combined all customer-facing resources into a single Global Sales and Marketing organization. This allowed the company to have a more efficient disciplined global approach to solve customer business needs and result in better planning and overall coordination. Today, Rockwell Automation has evolved from a product-centric company into a customer/market-centric company.

As the result of this focus, non-U.S. revenues as a percent of total sales grew from 33 percent in 2001 to almost 50 percent in 2007. The number of employees located outside of the U.S. grew from 29 percent to over 50 percent during that same period.

The company focused on expanding its presence worldwide – in Asia, Latin America, and other emerging international markets, such as Russia and Eastern Europe. In each of these regions, it introduced the Logix architecture and invested in new products, logistics, channel development and general management acumen, with the objective of positioning the business for long-term success.

Rockwell Automation also embarked on the next stage of globalizing its business model. This extends beyond sales and support activities and includes local business management, regional development resources, and infrastructure, all with the intention of bringing the company closer to its customers. To this end, the company established regional business centers and factories in China, Singapore, Poland and Mexico, each responsible for specific product lines.

Continued global expansion will be a key component of Rockwell Automation's ongoing transformation.

Driving Growth Through Acquisitions and Creation of a Pure-Play Enterprise

While organic growth has been a consistent underpinning of the company's success, strategic acquisitions and divestitures also have played a meaningful role in Rockwell Automation's transformation into what it is today – the largest "pure play" industrial automation company in the world.

To this end, Rockwell Automation sold its electronic commerce business in 2004 and, in 2006, sold the Rockwell Scientific Company, the R&D service provider it owned jointly with Rockwell Collins, to Teledyne Technologies. In 2007, Baldor Electric acquired Rockwell Automation's Dodge mechanical and Reliance Electric motors and motor repair services businesses, known collectively as Power Systems.

The divestiture of Power Systems – representing nearly $1 billion in revenue and a long-time mainstay business of the company – was a highly visible statement of Rockwell Automation's commitment to integrated architecture and intelligent motor control as the future of its value creation for shareholders and customers.

At the time of the divestiture of Power Systems, Rockwell Automation introduced two new reporting segments that represent the company today: Architecture & Software and Control Products & Solutions. The Architecture & Software segment contains all the elements of the company's integrated control and information architecture capable of connecting customers' entire manufacturing enterprise. The Control Products & Solutions segment combines a comprehensive portfolio of intelligent motor control and industrial control products, along with the customer support and application knowledge necessary to implement an automation or information solution.

Rockwell Automation has viewed acquisitions as an important element of its growth strategy. It is focused on businesses that expand its product and services breadth and scale, its technology capabilities and its global reach. Since 2001, the company has made 12 acquisitions, and each of these has accomplished one or more of these objectives. Each one has allowed Rockwell Automation to do more for its customers as well as expand its served market.

In 2007, Rockwell Automation took a more aggressive posture on acquisitions to act as a catalyst for additional growth. It put in place a new process to identify and prioritize a broader universe of potential acquisition candidates that will complement and accelerate the activities of its organic growth initiatives.

ROCKWELL AUTOMATION CONCLUSION

In the early 1970s, Allen-Bradley was at the forefront of the industry with its electro-mechanical products. In the 1980s, it led the move toward programmable logic controllers. In the 1990s, it spearheaded the movement to software, services and solutions. And the first decade of the 21st Century has been defined by its introduction of networked capabilities and information management across the enterprise.

Today, as an increasingly intellectual capital business, the vast majority of its value is based on people, technology, domain expertise and knowledge. This continued evolution of the company starts with technology leadership and focusing that leadership on innovation. That innovation allows Rockwell Automation to create differentiation for its customers. Differentiation defines long-term value both for the company's customers and shareowners, which drives loyalty ending with growth that allows the cycle to begin all over again with investment in new technology.

Throughout the many changes transformation of this magnitude involves, the original precepts of the Rockwell Vision and Credo linger. At Rockwell Automation, the vision remains focused on technology leadership and innovation and is supported by a fundamental set of core values that drive the company toward realization of that vision. The vision and values are priority messages that are woven into various media and actively demonstrated by leaders and employees on a daily basis. The values of innovation, customer focus, relentless pursuit of excellence, and speed are the cornerstones of the company's go-to-market messaging, and the Listen.Think.Solve. tagline used in external, customer-facing marketing materials supports the emphasis on those values.

Above all, Rockwell Automation has some of the best people in the world, and it is the combined force of the vision, values, leadership and people that gives the company a sustainable competitive advantage and drive long-term value creation in the marketplace. As a result of its ongoing transformation, Rockwell Automation continues to define the future growth of industrial automation – integrated, intelligent, and global. (www.rockwellautomation.com)

SHAREOWNER PERFORMANCE THROUGH THIS TRANSFORMATION

The table and chart below depict the results to the Rockwell shareowner who kept their shares resulting from all of the strategic transactions. The results assume only that any dividends received were reinvested in the respective stocks. During this almost 30-year period ending in September 2007, the shareowners achieved a 15.9 percent return compared to 12.8 percent from the S&P 500 computed on the same basis. Because of the major 2008 stock market performance, August 2008 also is shown. It is important to note that the real performance of the businesses continue much stronger than the stock market performance. Rockwell Automation and Rockwell Collins, in particular, continue to produce improved results.

Table 3 **Rockwell Returns - 1/1/79 to 9/30/07 and 8/31/08**
("Sum of the Parts")

	Rockwell		**S&P 500**	
	9/30/07	8/31/08	9/30/07	8/31/08
Investment at 1/1/79	$100	$100	$100	$100
Total Value	$8,458	$5,910	$3,645	$3,063
Increase in Value	85X	59X	36X	31X
Cumulative Average Annual Return	15.9%	14.1%	12.8%	11.8%

Note: Value of Rockwell assumes shares of Rockwell and all shares received from spin-offs held from time received. Value of Rockwell and S&P 500 assumes all cash dividends immediately reinvested.

Chart 16 below shows the same results year by year. The big spike in the 1999 period reflects the Internet bubble. The sharp rise in recent years reflects the stellar performance of Rockwell Collins and Rockwell Automation.

Chart 16 **Rockwell Stock Performance vs. S&P 500**

Value of $100 Investment

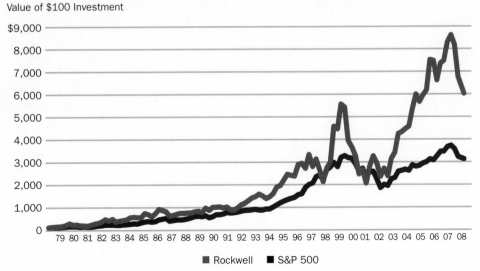

■ Rockwell   ■ S&P 500

The Rockwell shareowners who kept all the various securities that resulted from the strategic transactions as of May 2008, hold shares in Rockwell Automation (ROK), Rockwell Collins (COL), ArvinMeritor (ARM), Boeing (BA), Conexant (CNXT), Skyworks (SWKS), and Mindspeed (MSPD). The value of a Rockwell share held prior to the 1996 Boeing transaction can be computed as: $(1.0)(ROK+COL) + (0.1)(CNXT) + (0.084)(BA) + (0.25)(ARM) + (0.341)(SWKS) + (0.067)(MSPD)$. That value as of September 30, 2007, was about $160 (excluding dividends). That value had fallen to about $113 at August 31, 2008.

This is a situation where the math is correct but leaves one with the impression that Rockwell Automation and Rockwell Collins account for most of the current value. As noted several times in this book, one needs to recognize the tremendous importance of the contributions of the other businesses, particularly Aerospace in providing the cash and capital structure for Automation and Collins to be launched as public companies. For example, well over $3 billion was utilized to acquire Allen-Bradley, Reliance Electric and smaller acquisitions for Rockwell Automation. Additionally, over $5 billion was used to repurchase stock in the '90s that recapitalized the company, allowing all of the spun businesses to start with strong balance sheets and much lower outstanding shares.

CONCLUDING REMARKS

Thus, we have seen the formation of the major predecessor companies that came together to become Rockwell. We have seen the transformation of Rockwell from a 1960s conglomerate to become a diversified, high technology enterprise serving aerospace, electronics, and automotive global markets. We have learned how the leaders and the people of Rockwell developed and implemented management processes and put in place a set of values, attitudes and action strategies that resulted in a culture of strategic innovation and entrepreneurship. And, we have seen how the transformation of Rockwell brought value to the shareowner. Through a series of strategic transactions, the company became several market-focused businesses and, in the process, significant value was achieved for the Rockwell shareowner.

These businesses all benefited significantly from the values, management processes, training and entrepreneurial approach that was common to all Rockwell businesses. The management teams that lead all these newly independent businesses were almost exclusively from the Rockwell ranks and performed well. Some were in great markets and had stellar results. Some were in markets with more challenges and their potential has not yet been reached. The overall results have been impressive by any measure.

The performance of these leaders and their companies was addressed recently by Don Beall when he said, "Rockwell was built upon its predecessors – people and companies. The successors have taken the businesses to new heights, and they have my full confidence in their people, their values and their drive in always moving to the next level. Rockwell businesses have made many important contributions. It has been a privilege to have led this great company for so many years."

Biographies

60. Willard F. (Al) Rockwell, Jr.
president and chairman, Rockwell
Standard Corporation; president,
Rockwell Manufacturing Company;
president, North American Rockwell;
chairman, Rockwell International
Corporation

Willard F. (Al) Rockwell, Jr.

Willard Frederick Rockwell, Jr., known to many as Al, achieved prominence as the chairman of Rockwell International Corporation, which he fashioned through the merger of Rockwell Standard Corporation, Rockwell Manufacturing Company, North American Aviation, Collins Radio and other firms. He was actively involved during Rockwell International's participation in the Apollo Space Program and the company's leading role in the development of the space shuttle. He served as chairman of Rockwell International until his retirement in 1979, and as a board member until 1984.

Mr. Rockwell was born in Boston and grew up there and in Pittsburgh. He received an engineering degree of Penn State University in 1935. While attending Penn State, he became a member of the Kappa Sigma Fraternity and in 1992 was given the Man of the Century Award of the Kappa Sigma Fraternity, Alpha Delta Chapter. He served in World War II as an Army captain.

His career began in 1935 when he became an executive of the Timken-Detroit Axle Company, which his father had reorganized. Its name was later changed to Rockwell Standard. Mr. Rockwell returned to Pittsburgh from Detroit to work at Equitable Meter, a company that evolved into the Rockwell Manufacturing Company.

Eventually, Mr. Rockwell became president of both Rockwell Standard and Rockwell Manufacturing. He merged Rockwell Standard with North American Aviation to form North American Rockwell, then added Rockwell Manufacturing to create Rockwell International.

Previously, Mr. Rockwell was chairman and chief executive officer of Astrotech International Corporation and Space Shuttle of America Corporation, an Astrotech subsidiary, since joining Astrotech in September 1981. Strongly committed to the concept of commercialization and privatization of space, he was honored for his contributions to the U.S. space program, including awards from the American Astronautical Society in 1971 and, in 1982, the Bronze Medal of Honor from the International Institute of Technology, that organization's highest honor.

He was active in numerous international, national and local groups, including the Conference Board and the Allegheny Conference on Community Development in Pittsburgh. He also served on many boards of community organizations and universities. He received six honorary doctorates, as well as awards from the American Management Association and the United Negro College Fund.

Mr. Rockwell died on September 24, 1992, at the age of 78.

John Leland (Lee) Atwood

John Leland (Lee) Atwood joined North American Aviation Inc. in 1934, one year before the firm moved from Dundalk, Maryland, to Southern California. He previously worked at Douglas Aircraft in Southern California, builder of such venerable transports as the DC-3, so he would cross the country twice in a short time.

He soon became a vice president and, in 1938, was named assistant general manager of the company. In 1941, he became first vice president; in 1948 he was elected president; in 1960 he became chief executive officer at the retirement of Dutch Kindelberger; and in 1962 he became chairman of the board.

Mr. Atwood was born in Walton, Kentucky, on Oct. 26, 1904. He attended Hardin-Simmons University from 1924 to 1926, receiving a bachelor of arts degree, then completed postgraduate engineering courses at the University of Texas, earning a bachelor of science degree in 1928.

61. John Leland (Lee) Atwood, president, chief executive officer, chairman of the board, North American Aviation; president, chief executive officer, North American Rockwell

A number of leaders in the aerospace industry have described Mr. Atwood as "a chief engineer's chief engineer." His technical acumen was the driving force behind the company's evolution into an aviation and space leader that produced more military aircraft than any other company (a record which stands to this day). Among those aircraft: the P-51 Mustang, a swift, agile World War II fighter with an especially impressive record in the aerial war in Europe; the B-25 Mitchell bomber, used by Jimmy Doolittle and his Tokyo Raiders to turn the tide of the war in the Pacific; the T-6 Texan, which almost every U.S. and British WWII pilot trained in; and the F-86 Sabre Jet fighter, which exhibited a superiority of 10-to-1 or better against Russian MiGs in Korea.

As the company's aviation leadership continued after WWII, Mr. Atwood used his technical vision and managerial skills to establish his company as an indispensable national asset in new high-technology fields such as rocket propulsion, intercontinental ballistic missiles, and the Apollo moon-landing program.

In 1967, Mr. Atwood merged North American with Rockwell of Pittsburgh to form North American Rockwell (later to become Rockwell International). During the consolidation, he provided leadership in his role as president and chief executive officer of the new corporation, setting the stage for the company's continuing aerospace leadership as producers of the Space Shuttle and the B-1 bomber.

Mr. Atwood retired in 1970, but remained on the board of directors until 1978. Even after that, he maintained an active involvement with the company and its programs, and the company continued to regard him as an invaluable resource.

Under Mr. Atwood's leadership, the company and its employees captured three Collier Trophies, the aerospace industry's most prestigious awards, for their work on the F-100 supersonic fighter, the X-15 spaceplane, and the B-1 bomber.

Among numerous individual honors and awards bestowed on Mr. Atwood were a Presidential Citation from Harry S Truman for his contributions during WWII; the Air Force Association's Hap Arnold Trophy; and the Wright Brothers Memorial Trophy, awarded by the National Aeronautic Association. That association honored him again at a later date, declaring him an "Elder Statesman of Aviation" in ceremonies in 1976. Mr. Atwood also was an honorary fellow of the American Institute of Aeronautics and Astronautics – that organization's highest rank.

Mr. Atwood died on March 5, 1999, at the age of 94.

See also: http://www.boeing.com/news/feature/atwood/index.html

62. Robert (Bob) Anderson
chairman emeritus
Rockwell International Corporation

Robert Anderson

Robert Anderson was widely recognized for his strong leadership in the aerospace and defense and automotive industries. He retired from Rockwell in 1988 after serving 18 years in the two top executive positions: elected president and chief operating officer in 1970, and then chairman and chief executive officer in 1979. He was named chairman Emeritus in 1990 and had served on the Board as a director from 1968 to 1990.

At the height of his tenure at Rockwell, company sales exceeded $10 billion with more than 125,000 employees in its aerospace, electronics, automotive, and general businesses. Also during Anderson's tenure, Rockwell was the prime contractor for five of the six space shuttles. He forged strong ties with the Reagan administration, which benefited the company in 1981, when the Defense Department revived a plan to build 100 B-1 bombers – supersonic, swing-wing jets designed to elude radar by flying at low altitudes to deliver nuclear warheads. Mr. Anderson had learned to fly so that he could relate to the Air Force officers more clearly during the company's efforts to get the B-1 revived. The B-1 bomber program was completed when the 100th bomber rolled off the production line in the spring of 1988.

Born in Nebraska on Nov. 2, 1920, Mr. Anderson earned a bachelor's degree in mechanical engineering from Colorado State University in 1943. He served as a captain in the United States Army Field Artillery until 1946.

Following his military service, Mr. Anderson spent 22 years with Chrysler Corporation where his career at the auto company included increasingly important executive positions in engineering, product planning, manufacturing, and marketing. He earned a master's degree in automotive engineering from the Chrysler Institute of Engineering. While at Chrysler, Mr. Anderson was an active member of the Society of Automotive Engineers (SAE) as chairman of its Detroit section in 1963 and 1964, and chairman of the SAE's Engineering Activity Board in 1967.

Mr. Anderson participated in the development of the powerful "426 Hemi" engine for use by NASCAR racing great Richard Petty, who in 1964 won his first Daytona 500 race driving a Plymouth "hemi." Plymouth finished 1-2-3 in that race. He also was instrumental in creating and marketing the Plymouth Road Runner, a successful production "muscle" car in its day.

Among his many honors and awards, Mr. Anderson received during his career was an honorary doctor of law degree in 1966 from Colorado State University and a subsequent presentation from his alma mater in 1967 of its Honor Achievement Award for "outstanding scholastic and professional achievement." That same year, his native state designated him as "one of Nebraska's 100 distinguished citizens."

Mr. Anderson was a member of the board of governors of the Aerospace Industries Association of America (AIA) and its chairman in 1978. He also served as a member of the board of the John Anderson Graduate School of Management at UCLA, as well as the California Institute of Technology at Pasadena, CA, and a board director at Aurora Capital Group and at Roller Bearing Corporation. In addition, Mr. Anderson was a member and past chairman of the Conquistadores del Cielo; and the Bohemian Club of San Francisco. He also served on the board of directors for Celanese, Owens-Illinois; and the Hospital Corporation of America.

He was the national chairman of the United Nations Day for two successive years, and was honored for his chairmanship in June 1989.

Mr. Anderson died in October 2006 at the age of 85, following a long, successful – and quite historic – career. He is survived by Diane Anderson, his wife whom he married in 1973; two children, Dr. Robert Anderson, Jr. of Blaine, WA, and Kathleen (Kit) Thomas of Vancouver, BC; two stepchildren, Keri Anderson of Brentwood, CA, and Erin Anderson of Tarzana, CA, and four grandchildren.

Donald R. Beall

Don retired from Rockwell in 1998 after a 30-year career. He served as chairman/CEO or president/COO for 20 years. Rockwell was a global leader in aerospace, electronics and automotive markets. Through a series of strategic actions, the company became focused on a diversified group of leadership electronics businesses serving factory automation, communications, avionics and various communications-semiconductor world markets. Those electronics businesses today are represented by five public companies through which significant shareowner value has been created.

Don serves as a director on the boards of Rockwell Collins and CT Realty. He is a former director of Conexant Systems, Mindspeed Technologies, Jazz Semiconductors, Skyworks Solutions, Proctor and Gamble, Amoco, Rockwell and Times Mirror. Currently, he is a partner in Dartbrook Partners (a family partnership) and the chairman of the Beall Family Foundation. His wife, Joan, and their two sons, Jeff and Ken, are active in the management of both Dartbrook Partners and the Beall Family Foundation. The Beall Family Foundation has endowed the Don Beall Dean of Engineering at San Jose State University, the Don Beall Center for Innovation and Entrepreneurship at the UCI Paul Merage School of Management, and the Donald R. Beall Chair in Strategic Management at the University of Pittsburgh.

Don is very involved with the University of California Irvine. He is a member of the UCI Paul Merage School of Business Dean's Advisory Board, the Executive Committee, and the Don Beall Center for Innovation and Entrepreneurship Advisory Board; the UCI Henry Samueli School of Engineering Advisory Board; UCI Beall Center for Arts & Technology Advisory Board, and the UCI Chief Executive Roundtable. He is also on the Advisory Board for the Cal-(IT)2, a major UCI/UCSD research project. He is an advisor to the San Jose State University School of Engineering and member of the Engineering Leadership Council; a trustee and President's Circle member of the Naval Postgraduate School Foundation. He is also an Overseer of the Hoover institution at Stanford; a member of the Business Executives for National Security; on the Presidents' Circle of National Academies of Science, Engineering & Medicine; a member of numerous Young Presidents Organization alumni groups; member and past chairman of the Conquistadores del Cielo; the Old Capital Club of Monterey; and the Bohemian Club of San Francisco. He is a Fellow of the American Institute of Aeronautics and Astronautics and was a trustee of the California Institute of Technology for many years. Mr. Beall was a member of the board of governors of the Aerospace Industries Association of America (AIA) and a past chairman. Mr. Beall also serves on the board of directors for the Saint Joseph's Ballet, a community organization that seeks to build the self-esteem of inner-city youth.

In 1998, Don and his wife, Joan, were recognized by Rockwell through the funding of the establishment of the UCI Donald R. Beall and Joan F. Beall Center for Art and Technology. Other recent honors include: 2001 UCI Medal (awarded to Don and Joan individually); 1998 Horatio Alger Award; 1996 Human Relations Award from the Orange County Chapter of the American Jewish Committee, shared with his wife, Joan; and 1996 Front & Center Award as Orange County Person of the Year, given by CSU, Fullerton. Don has an engineering degree from San Jose and a MBA from the University of Pittsburgh. San Jose State University and the University of Pittsburgh Joseph M. Katz Graduate School of Business have honored Mr. Beall with distinguished alumnus awards. Don also received the 1991 Exemplary Leadership in Management Award from the John E. Anderson School of Management, UCLA. He is involved in numerous professional, educational, public service and philanthropic endeavors and is an investor, director, and/or advisor with several venture capital groups, individual companies and investment partnerships.

Beall has been married for 47 years to Joan Beall. They have two married sons, and two grand-daughters and three grandsons. Don and Joan reside in Corona del Mar and Pebble Beach, CA.

63. Donald R. Beall
chairman emeritus
retired chairman & chief executive officer, Rockwell
partner, Dartbrook Partners, LLC (a family partnership)

64. Don H Davis, Jr.
chairman emeritus
Rockwell Automation

Don H. Davis, Jr.

Don H. Davis, Jr., is chairman emeritus of Rockwell Automation, a position he has held since February 2005. In February 2007, after serving for 12 years, Davis retired from the Rockwell Automation board of directors. Davis previously served as chairman and CEO of Rockwell Automation since 1998.

Davis, who joined Allen-Bradley in 1963 (acquired by Rockwell in 1985) as an engineering sales trainee, has held a series of key corporate and business unit executive positions within the company.

Davis joined the Allen-Bradley Sales Division in 1963 and was steadily appointed to posts of greater responsibility. In 1966, he became a district manager for the company's sales office in Birmingham, Alabama. In 1979, Davis was appointed general manager of the Allen-Bradley Programmable Controller Division. A year later, he was named vice president of that unit. He became vice president and general manager of the Industrial Control Division in 1982.

Davis was promoted to senior vice president at Allen-Bradley in 1985 and became head of the Industrial Control Group in 1986. In 1987, Davis was named senior vice president and general manager of the Industrial Computer and Communication Group, and in 1989 he was appointed president of Allen-Bradley.

As president of Allen-Bradley, Davis provided the leadership for significant growth outside the United States, as well as the establishment of a number of successful commercial initiatives (e.g., partnerships/alliances, global accounts program), which created the foundation for what has become Rockwell Automation, the world's leading automation supplier. Prior to his role as chairman and CEO, Davis served as executive vice president and chief operating officer with responsibility for Rockwell International's automation, former semiconductor systems, and automotive components businesses.

Davis earned a bachelor's degree in mechanical engineering and master's degree from Texas A&M University. Davis is a member of the board of directors of Illinois Tool Works. He is a former member of the Business Council, The Conference Board and the Business Roundtable. Davis is also a former Board member of the Medical College of Wisconsin, the CIENA Corporation, the Museum of Science and Industry, Journal Communications, Rockwell Scientific and Apogent. He also is past chairman of the Board of Governors of the National Electrical Manufacturers Association, Washington, DC, and Big Brothers Big Sisters of Greater Milwaukee.

An active supporter of education and community programs, Davis served on the board of the Business Committee for the Arts and as a regent for the Milwaukee School of Engineering. He is also a former member of a number of educational and civic councils including the Greater Milwaukee Committee, and Boys and Girls Clubs of America. He is also the former chairman of the Midwest Region of the Boys and Girls Clubs of America and is now appointed to lifetime Governor Emeritus for that organization. Davis was co-chairman for the 2002 United Way Campaign of Greater Milwaukee, and was also co-chairman for the 2000 United Performing Arts Fund (UPAF) campaign.

Davis has been married for over 40 years to Sallie Davis, with 3 married sons and 3 grand-daughters, residing in Whitefish Bay, WI and Sedona, AZ.

APPENDIX 1

THE LEADERS

After the 1967 NAA/Rockwell merger, W. F. (Al) Rockwell, Jr. was chairman and J. Leland (Lee) Atwood was president and CEO. Rockwell had led Rockwell Standard, and Atwood had led NAA for many years. Robert Anderson was recruited from Chrysler to head what had been Rockwell Standard. Wallace Booth was recruited from Ford to be the Chief Financial Officer. John Moore, another long-time NAA executive, headed the NAA businesses. Atwood retired after a couple of years, and Anderson became president and CEO. Anderson was a seasoned general manager and a strong leader. He immersed himself in the Aerospace business, became a pilot, and was very "hands-on," particularly with the major Aerospace programs and customers. Al Rockwell encouraged many acquisitions, such as Miehle Goss Dexter (newspaper printing presses), numerous textile machinery businesses, Rockwell Manufacturing (a separate company in power tools, gas and water meters, oil field and power generation valves, etc.) … all very much in the diversification/conglomeration mode. Robert Wilson (recruited from General Electric) replaced Anderson to head the commercial businesses and subsequently led Collins for a short time before leaving to become the CEO of Memorex. Don Beall was recruited from Philco-Ford in 1968 to lead the Financial Planning efforts for the new company with the understanding that he would move into general management after one year.

After a series of General Manager assignments (including president of Collins), Beall was made president and COO in 1979; Anderson became chairman and CEO; and Rockwell retired. Martin (Skip) Walker was an executive vice president with responsibility for the Automotive and certain other commercial businesses. All of the Aerospace, Electronics and Energy businesses reported directly to Beall, as did Walker. Anderson retired in 1988, and Beall became chairman and CEO. The Aerospace and Electronics key executives during the '80s and '90s included George Jeffs, a great leader of the Space programs (Apollo, Shuttle, GPS, and many other initiatives). He also was a leading force in the important SDI (Strategic Defense Initiatives). Buzz Hello and Sam Iacobellis were leaders in the Aircraft and Space business. Sam became "Mr. B-1" as the leader of one of DOD's (Department of Defense) most successful major aerospace endeavors. Sam subsequently led all of the aerospace businesses. Art Ronan, Ron Roudebusch, and Larry Yost were leaders or the Automotive businesses. Larry became the first chairman/CEO of what became ArvinMeritor to be succeeded by Charles (Chip) McClure.

Kent Black came up through Collins and Electronics and became one of the EVPs accountable for Aerospace and Electronics. Other leaders in the Aerospace and Electronics businesses included Don Yockey and John McLuckey, a financial executive who became one of the most effective business leaders. Dwight Decker followed Lanny Ross as head of the Semiconductor businesses and later became CEO of Conexant. Scott Mercer now leads Conexant. Dave Aldrich leads Skyworks, and Raouf Halim leads Mindspeed. Clay Jones moved from very effective leadership of the company's Washington Office to become a GM under Jack Cosgrove at Collins. He rose steadily to become chairman/CEO of Rockwell Collins.

Allen-Bradley had outstanding management. At the time of the Acquisition of Allen-Bradley, Tracy O'Rourke was CEO and became one of the Corporate EVPs. Don Davis succeeded him as president of Allen-Bradley and was steadily promoted to become president and COO under Beall. Davis succeeded Beall as CEO in 1997, leading the new Rockwell, the diversified Electronics company. Davis was a key player in all of the strategic moves in the '90s and very effectively led the new company. Keith Nosbusch became president of Allen-Bradley and is now chairman/CEO of Rockwell Automation.

After Booth, Bob DePalma became CFO, followed by Mike Barnes. John Roscia was General Counsel, followed by Charlie Harff and Bill Calise. Charlie played a very crucial role in all of the big decisions of the '80s and '90s. In Human Resources, Bob Murphy, Tom Sumrall, and Joel Stone played important roles. Other key players were Jim McDivitt in numerous important assignments, Tom Cambabosso, Dick Foxen, Bill Fletcher and Lon Kight in International and Jim Meechan, Bob Cattoi, Tom Gunckel, Joe Longo and Derek Cheung in Engineering and the Rockwell Science Center. Sam Petok, Dick Mau and Earl Washington led Communications, and Ed Loeser and Dick Bohlen were among the leaders of Operations.

One is hesitant to list so many important team contributors knowing that so many unnamed were equally crucial to the company's many accomplishment.

From the Flip Phone Through the Backbone

Every message that travels through the Internet navigates two basic layers of infrastructure equipment before entering the high-speed optical core, and the same two layers on the way out. Conexant's semiconductor system solutions are used at each end of that process, and at every major step in between

PERSONAL NETWORKING

Access Edge

Aggrega

Users have more ways to create and send messages, faxes, emails, and images, and they have better ways to connect – including BLUETOOTH™ technology for wirelessly linking PCs, digital cameras and other communications devices to each other and the Internet in the

broadband digital home. The messages are collected at the access edge and formatted for transport across the network. Conexant routing software, packet processors and low-speed T/E carrier and DSL physical-layer (PHY) devices are used to create the

Personal Devices

PC

TV

PDA

Cell Phone

Mobile Internet Terminal

Access Edge Equipment
Cable Head End
Digital Carrier
Branch Office Router
T1/E1 DSL IAD

Aggregation E

ACQUISITIONS

Conexant acquired 10 companies during fiscal 2000 that extended our portfolio of products for personal networking devices and Internet infrastructure equipment

Philsar Semiconductor, Inc. - BLUETOOTH RF

Sierra Imaging, Inc. - Camera Back-End Software

Maker Communications, Inc. - Network Processor

NetPlane Systems, Inc. - Protocol Stacks and Network Control Software

Applied Telecom, Inc. - Physical-Layer Software

Microcosm Communica

Creation Strategy

CONEXANT®
BROADBAND COMMUNICATIONS

Dial-up Access Solutions

Broadband Access Solutions

- Most comprehensive end-to-end portfolio of broadband communications products and technologies
- Key leadership positions in dial-up and broadband modems, home networking processors, set-top box systems and components

...The Final Step

MNDSPEED™
INTERNET INFRASTRUCTURE

Multiservice Access Solutions

T/E Carrier Products

Network Processors

- Internet infrastructure business of Conexant
- Core product franchises have leadership positions in metro/access markets
- Complementary product offerings include a broad range of switching and transmission products
- Scheduled to be spun off when business and market conditions permit

The world of communications has become a very big place. As the industry has grown, it has also evolved, dividing itself into a number of sizable wireless and wireline market segments, each with its own unique characteristics and requirements. In response, Conexant has taken its strengths as one of the world's largest and oldest communications semiconductor suppliers, and redeployed them across a family of focused pure-play companies.

Focused Business

Conexant has created four companies that have solid leadership positions in a substantial, fast-growing communications market.

C O N E X A N T®

PERSONAL NETWORKING, INTERNET INFRASTRUCTURE, WAFER MANUFACTURING

SiRF®
GLOBAL POSITIONING SYSTEMS

- Transaction completed in September 2001
- Merged Conexant's global positioning system (GPS) business with SiRF
- Privately held
- Created largest pure-play GPS semiconductor player, enabling products that deliver instant location information

JAZZ
SEMICONDUCTOR
SPECIALTY SEMICONDUCTOR FOUNDRY

- Transaction completed in March 2002
- Conexant partnered with The Carlyle Group to create privately held company
- Conexant's former Newport Beach wafer fabrication facility is centerpiece
- World's first pure-play mixed-signal and radio-frequency (RF) wafer manufacturing foundry

SKYWORKS™
WIRELESS

- Transaction completed in June 2002
- Conexant spun wireless business and merged with Alpha Industries, Inc.
- Publicly held
- Pure-play leader in front-end modules, RF subsystems and complete cellular systems for wireless handsets and infrastructure

pictos™
DIGITAL IMAGING

- Transaction completed in July 2002
- Conexant privatized digital imaging business and merged with Zing Network
- Privately held, backed by $17 million funding round led by Kleiner Perkins Caufield & Byers
- Offers broadest portfolio for developing digital cameras and imaging-enabled mobile communications products

Appendix 2
Focused Business Creation Strategy

Focused Business Creation Strategy better explains the opportunity as well as risk of the broad Conexant strategy.

NETWORK   INFRASTRUCTURE

tion

Optical Transport

Aggregation

systems that process these messages. The messages from many customers are combined onto higher-bit-rate trunks for efficient transport across the Internet. Conexant's multiservice access processors, DSL products, OC-3/OC-12 PHY devices and network processors all play a role here in the aggregation edge, which is the principle service-deployment loca-

The messages travel through the carrier's increasingly all-optical infrastructure at near-lightspeed data rates. Conexant provides a variety of critical products for the equipment used here, including laser drivers, high-speed OC-12 and OC-48 SONET framers, and an expanding portfolio of system chips such as our OC-192 crosspoint switch.

tion fo
As the
tion, ag
de-mu.
speed
data ra
used in
centers
(POPs
OptiPH
age a l
width s

		Optical Transport Equipment	Gateway Router	Aggregation Equipment	Edge
uipment	DSLAM		Terabit Router		ATM
	Remote Access Concentrator		SONET Add/Drop Multiplexer		Subs
	Voice/Data Gateway		Cross-Connect Optical Switch		Cent
			DWDM Transport		Multi
					Fram

ons Limited - Optical

Novanet Semiconductor | Ltd. - SONET

HotRail Inc. - Switch Fabric

Appendix 3
From the Flip Phone Through the Backbone
A characterization of Conexant products

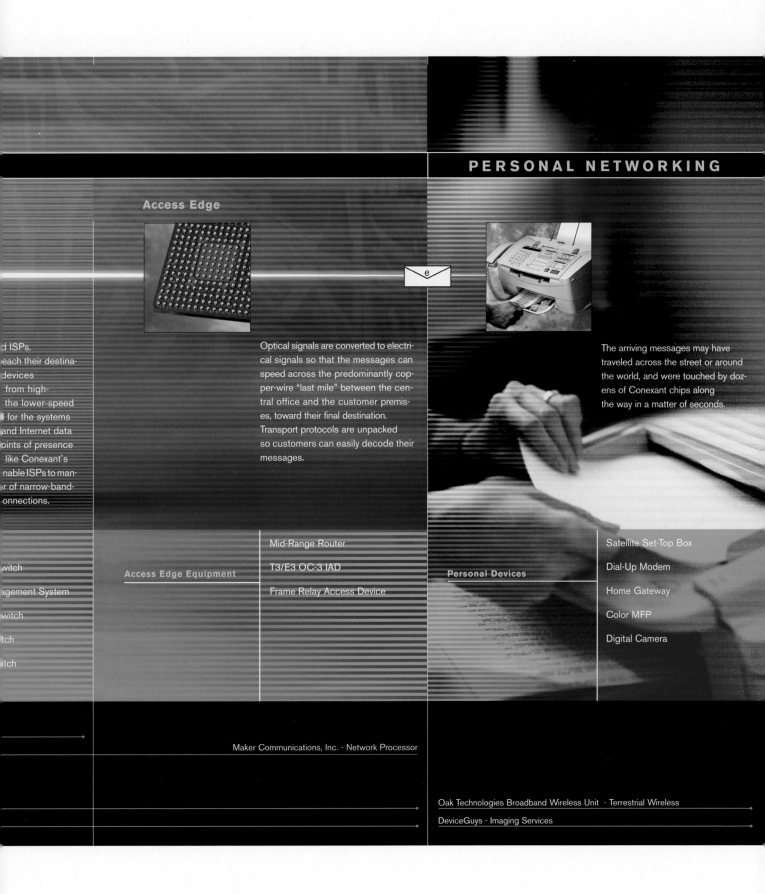

PERSONAL NETWORKING

Access Edge

Optical signals are converted to electrical signals so that the messages can speed across the predominantly copper-wire "last mile" between the central office and the customer premises, toward their final destination. Transport protocols are unpacked so customers can easily decode their messages.

d ISPs.

each their destina-
devices
from high-
the lower-speed
for the systems
and Internet data
oints of presence
like Conexant's
nable ISPs to man-
r of narrow-band-
onnections.

The arriving messages may have traveled across the street or around the world, and were touched by dozens of Conexant chips along the way in a matter of seconds.

Access Edge Equipment	
	Mid-Range Router
	T3/E3 OC-3 IAD
	Frame Relay Access Device

Personal Devices	
	Satellite Set-Top Box
	Dial-Up Modem
	Home Gateway
	Color MFP
	Digital Camera

witch
agement System
witch
tch
itch

Maker Communications, Inc. - Network Processor

Oak Technologies Broadband Wireless Unit - Terrestrial Wireless

DeviceGuys - Imaging Services

REFERENCES

1. Arthur Collins – Radio Wizard by Ben W. Stearns, Copyright 2002 Ben W. Stearns, ISBN 0-9716416-0-9

2. The Bradley Legacy – Lynde and Harry Bradley, Their Company, and Their Foundation by John Gurda, Copyright 1992, The Lynde and Harry Bradley Foundation, Library of Congress Catalog Card No. 92-81974

3. The First 50 Years – A History of Collins Radio Company and the Collins Divisions of Rockwell International by Ken C. Braband – with excerpts from articles by: Dr. R.L. Carrel, Arlo Goodyear, Tony Huebsch, Gerald Ozburn, Horst Schweighofer, John Staehle, and Ben Stearns, Copyright 1983 by the Communications Deparment, Avionics Group, Rockwell International, Cedar Rapids, Iowa

4. Lee Atwood … Dean of Aerospace by Russ Murray, Copyright 1980, Rockwell International Corporation

5. Rockwell – The Heritage of North American by Bill Yenne, Copyright 1989 Brompton Books Corp., ISBN 0-517-67252-9

6. North American Aviation, Inc. Evolution (historical timeline/chart and Operations History covering the years 1924 – 1965) NAA Publication 527-V Rev. 1-66

7. Evolution of a Space Capability – North American Aviation, Inc. (Historical Profile, including timeline/chart covering the years 1945 – 1962) NAA Publication No. New 54-W Rev. 6-1962

8. North American Aviation – A Legacy of Leadership by Jim Albaugh, The Boeing Company, published in North American Aviation Retirees Bulletin – A Bald Eagles Inc. Publication, Winter 2006

9. Summary Financial Information is available for each business spun off from Rockwell. This information will be updated every year by Dartbrook Partners, LLC (Mr. Beall's family partnership) at 5 San Joaquin Plaza #320, Newport Beach, CA 92660

10. Webcasts & Analyst Presentations

    a. www.arvinmeritor.com

    b. www.rockwellautomation.com

    c. www.boeing.com

    d. www.rockwellcollins.com

    e. www.conexant.com

    f. www.skyworks.com

    g. www.mindspeed.com

11. DVD – Junior Achievement – Donald R. Beall, 1993

12. DVD – Donald R. Beall Clips 1993 – 1997

13. DVD – Self-Made in California, Rockwell, 1997

14. DVD – Rockwell Management Meeting, 1997

The Paul Merage School of Business at the University of California, Irvine, is pleased to publish this book in honor of Don Beall, whose groundbreaking, innovative guidance transformed a company and is a model of effective corporate leadership. We are most grateful for his continued support and guidance.

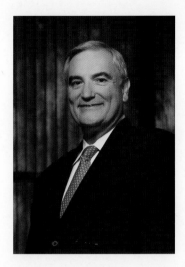

Dean Andrew J. Policano
The Paul Merage School of Business

About The Paul Merage School of Business

The Paul Merage School of Business at UC Irvine offers four dynamic MBA programs – plus PhD and undergraduate business degrees – that deliver its thematic approach to business education: sustainable growth through strategic innovation. We graduate leaders with the exceptional ability to help grow their organizations through analytical decision-making, advanced technology and collaborative execution. In-class and on-site experiences with real-world business problems give students the edge needed to help companies compete in today's global economy.

Six Centers of Excellence and an Executive Education program provide numerous and varied opportunities for students and the business community at large to enhance their education experience and update their professional expertise. While the Merage School is relatively young, it has quickly grown to consistently rank among the top 10% of all AACSB-accredited programs through exceptional student recruitment, world-class faculty, a strong alumni network and close individual and corporate relationships. The Merage School combines the academic strengths and best traditions of the University of California with the cutting-edge, entrepreneurial spirit of Orange County in the heart of America's Tech Coast.

About The Don Beall Center for Innovation and Entrepreneurship at The Paul Merage School of Business

The Don Beall Center for Innovation and Entrepreneurship provides a focal point to help business visionaries transfer their ideas into viable business opportunities, either in new ventures or within existing organizations. Through leadership, education, and potential partnerships, the Center creates an environment that fosters a connection among world-class UC Irvine researchers, innovative visionaries, savvy business leaders, creative venture capitalists and pivotal business channels.

This network also serves as a viable launching point for the next generation of management science and research on innovation and entrepreneurship. At the heart of the Center is its Innovation Knowledge Base with its objective to understand processes that minimize the randomness of business innovation through research, knowledge sharing and practical application. As such, the Center will be the vehicle through which a large proportion of research and thought leadership on the newest and most influential approaches to strategic innovation will be completed and disseminated to global business.

Learn more at merage.uci.edu and visit our Innovation Knowledge Base from the Beall Center at merage.uci.edu/go/innovation.